The Life in the Sonnets

A complete recording of the Sonnets, read by David Fuller, is available at http://www.continuumbooks.com/resources /9781847064547

Shakespeare

Shakespeare Now!
Series edited by Ewan Fernie and Simon Palfrey

First Wave:
At the Bottom of Shakespeare's Ocean Steve Mentz
Godless Shakespeare Eric S. Mallin
Shakespeare's Double Helix Henry S. Turner
Shakespeare Inside Amy Scott-Douglass
Shakespearean Metaphysics Michael Witmore
Shakespeare's Modern Collaborators Lukas Erne
Shakespeare Thinking Philip Davis
To Be Or Not To Be Douglas Bruster

Second Wave:
The King and I Philippa Kelly
The Life in the Sonnets David Fuller   ·
Hamlet's Dreams David Schalkwyk
Nine Lives of William Shakespeare Graham Holderness
Shakespeare and I edited by Theodora Papadopoulou and
   William McKenzie

The Life in the Sonnets

David Fuller

continuum

Continuum International Publishing Group

The Tower Building
11 York Road
London SE1 7NX

80 Maiden Lane
Suite 704
New York, NY 10038

www.continuumbooks.com

British Library Cataloguing-in-Publication Data
A catalogue record for this book is available from the British Library.

ISBN: 978-1-8470-6453-0 (hardback)
       978-1-8470-6454-7 (paperback)

Library of Congress Cataloging-in-Publication Data
Fuller, David, 1947-
The Life in the sonnets/David Fuller.
    p. cm. – (Shakespeare Now!)
Includes bibliographical references and index.
ISBN 978-1-84706-454-7 (pbk.) – ISBN 978-1-84706-453-0 (hardback)
1. Shakespeare, William, 1564–1616. Sonnets.
2. Sonnets, English–History and Criticism–Theory, etc. I. Title.

PR2848.F75 2011
821'.3–dc22   2010029091

Typeset by Newgen Imaging Systems Pvt Ltd, Chennai, India
Printed and bound in India by Replika Press Pvt Ltd

To Corinne

Contents

General Editors' Preface to the Second-Wave of the Series

We begin with the passions of the critic as they are forged and explored in Shakespeare. These books speak directly from that fundamental experience of losing and remaking yourself in art. This does not imply, necessarily, a lonely existentialism; the story of a self is always bound up in other stories, shared tales of nations or faiths, or of families large and small. But such stories are also always singular, irreducible to the generalities by which they are typically explained. Here, then, is where literary experience stops pretending to institutionalized objectivity, and starts to tell its own story.

Shakespeare Now! is a rallying cry, above all for aesthetic immediacy. It favours a model of aesthetic knowledge as *encounter*, where the encounter brings its own, often surprising contextualising imperatives. Implicit in this is the premise that art is as much a subject as an object, less like aggregated facts and more like a fascinating person or persons. And encountering the plays as such is unavoidably personal.

Much recent scholarship has been devoted to Shakespeare *then*—to producing more information about the presumed moment of their inception. But this moment of inception is in truth happening over and over, again and again, anywhere that Shakespeare is being experienced anew or freshly. For the fact is that he remains by a country mile, the most important *contemporary* writer—the most performed and read, the most written about, but also the most remembered. But it is not a question merely of Shakespeare in the present, as though his vitality is best measured by his passing relevance to great events. It is about his works' abiding *presence*.

In some ways, criticism needs to get younger—to recover the freshness of aesthetic experience, and so in part better to remember why any of us should care. We need a new directness, written responses to the plays which attest to the life we find in them and the life they find in us.

Ewan Fernie and Simon Palfrey

General Editors' Preface

Shakespeare Now! represents a new form for new approaches. Whereas academic writing is far too often ascendant and detached, attesting all too clearly to years of specialist training, *Shakespeare Now!* offers a series of intellectual adventure stories: animate with fresh and often exposed thinking, with ideas still heating in the mind.

This series of 'minigraphs' will thus help to bridge two yawning gaps in current public discourse. First, the gap between scholarly thinking and a public audience: the assumption of academics that they cannot speak to anyone but their peers unless they hopelessly dumb down their work. Second, the gap between public audience and scholarly thinking: the assumption of regular playgoers, readers, or indeed actors that academics write about the plays at a level of abstraction or specialization that they cannot hope to understand.

But accessibility should not be mistaken for comfort or predictability. Impatience with scholarly obfuscation is usually accompanied by a basic impatience with anything but (supposed) common sense. What this effectively means is a distrust of really thinking, and a disdain for anything that might unsettle conventional assumptions, particularly through crossing or re-drafting formal, political, or theoretical boundaries. We encourage such adventure, and base our claim to a broad audience upon it.

Here, then, is where our series is innovative: no compromising of the sorts of things that can be thought; a commitment to publishing powerful cutting-edge scholarship; but a conviction that these things are essentially communicable, that we can find a language that is enterprising, individual and shareable.

To achieve this we need a form that can capture the genuine challenge and vigour of thinking. Shakespeare is intellectually exciting, and so too are the ideas and debates that thinking about his work can provoke. But published scholarship often fails to communicate much of this. It is difficult to sustain excitement over the 80–120,000 words customary for a monograph: difficult enough for the writer, and perhaps even more so for the reader. Scholarly articles have likewise become a highly formalized mode not only of publication, but also of intellectual production. The brief length of articles means that a concept can be outlined, but its implications or application can rarely be tested in detail. The decline of sustained, exploratory attention to the singularity of a play's language, occasion, or movement is one of the unfortunate results. Often 'the play' is somehow assumed, a known and given thing that is not really worth exploring. So we spend our time pursuing collateral contexts: criticism becomes a belated, historicizing footnote.

Important things have got lost. Above all, any vivid sense as to why we are bothered with these things in the first place? Why read? Why go to plays? Why are they important? How does any pleasure they give relate to any of the things we labour to say about them? In many ways, literary criticism has forgotten affective and political immediacy. It has assumed a shared experience of the plays and then averted the gaze from any such experience, or any testing of it. We want a more ductile and sensitive mode of production; one that has more chance of capturing what people are really thinking and reading about, rather than what the pre-empting imperatives of journal or respectable monograph tend to encourage.

Furthermore, there is a vast world of intellectual possibility – from the past and present – that mainstream Shakespeare criticism has all but ignored. In recent years there has been a move away from 'theory' in literary studies: an aversion to its obscure jargon and complacent self-regard; a sense that its tricks were too easily rehearsed and that the whole game has become one of diminishing returns. This has further encouraged a retreat into the supposed safety of historicism. Of course the best of such work is stimulating, revelatory, and indispensable. But too often there is little trace of any struggle; little sense that the writer is coming at the subject afresh, searching for the most appropriate language or method. Alternatively, the prose is so laboured that all trace of an urgent story is quite lost.

We want to open up the sort of thinking – and thinkers – that might help us get at what Shakespeare is doing or why Shakespeare matters. This might include psychology, cognitive science, theology, linguistics, phenomenology, metaphysics, ecology, history, political theory; it can mean other art forms such as music, sculpture, painting, dance; it can mean the critical writing itself becomes a creative act.

In sum, we want the minigraphs to recover what the Renaissance 'essay' form was originally meant to embody. It meant an 'assay' – a trial or a test of something; putting something to the proof; and doing so in a form that is not closed-off and that cannot be reduced to a system. We want to communicate intellectual activity at its most alive: when it is still exciting to the one doing it; when it is questing and open, just as Shakespeare is. Literary criticism – that is, really thinking about words in action, plays as action – can start making a much more creative and vigorous contribution to contemporary intellectual *life*.

Simon Palfrey and Ewan Fernie

Acknowledgements

I am grateful to Kevin Billington for the very kind loan of copies of his 1983–84 television films of readings and discussions of the Sonnets; to Ron Berry and Martin Allison of Durham University's Department of Music for their invaluable assistance with recording the Sonnets; to Professor José Ramón Díaz Fernández for a session he organized on Shakespeare and Film at the Conference of the European Society for the Study of English in Zaragoza in 2004 at which I was able to try out some preliminary ideas about Derek Jarman; and to Dr Oliver Taylor for the reference to D. H. Lawrence on reading aloud (pp. 101–2).

Anna Fleming and Colleen Coalter at Continuum, and Mr P. Muralidharan and his production team at Newgen Imaging Systems, could not have been more pleasant to work with. Ewan Fernie and Simon Palfrey, as only begetters and general editors of *Shakespeare Now!*, have been ideally both permissive and demanding.

I owe a more personal debt to Michael Schepers, who, over many years, has responded to and commented vigorously on matters of life and art particularly relevant to part one. A yet more comprehensive debt to Corinne Saunders, for the most delightful forms of encouragement, support, and commentary, is acknowledged by the dedication.

Prologue

Literary criticism is a subject without boundaries. Anything can be relevant: the most precise terms of expression; formal or generic conventions; authors or audiences; abstruse learning or popular culture; the historical – knowledge of the other arts, society, intellectual or spiritual life, the history of particular meanings, or of how meanings were made; and the ahistorical – constructions of significance culturally remote from a work's point of origin, meanings determined by the needs and interests of present readers. And since art is emotional knowledge, criticism that is fully engaged will include, implicitly or explicitly, individual experience, a particular reader's cultural situation and personal values and ideas. 'There is', as T. S. Eliot puts it, 'no method except to be very intelligent'.

But institutional literary criticism is characteristically a subject with boundaries. Science sets its agendas – specialization, objectivity, progress models of knowledge. The institutional critic is a professional – a specialist (in a period or genre more or less sharply delineated: Romantic poetry, the 1790s), often with a method (deconstruction, new historicism), or a framing non-literary agenda (Marxism, feminism), and with a knowledge of the current (fashionable) state of opinion in his or her specialism: all ways of signifying membership of a professional group, and of allowing – even relying on – special knowledge to limit the demands on intelligence.

Special knowledge may indeed contribute to understanding, but only if it is recognized as preliminary and partial. Full engagement – understanding that both draws on and affects who we are and how we feel and act – is inherently more anarchic: its nature and needs are too various to fit within a critical programme, or even fully to be brought into consciousness. Real encounters with art involve an emotional openness which is the reverse of professional. Reporting that understanding means an adventure in thinking wherever feeling leads, an attitude that is fundamentally at odds with the quasi-scientific. Criticism needs to be more humble about the pretensions of intellect in relation to the splendour of the mysteries of art.

* * *

Damit es Kunst giebt, damit es irgend ein ästhetisches Thun und Schauen giebt, dazu ist eine physiologische Vorbedingung unumgänglich: der Rausch.

For art to exist, for any sort of aesthetic activity or perception to exist, a certain physiological precondition is necessary: intoxication.

(Nietzsche, *Twilight of the Idols*, 'Expeditions of an Untimely Man', 8.)

'Intoxication': deflection from the mind's normal state; diminished acknowledgement of the ordinary and contingent; heightened aware-ness of what is extraordinary, below the surface, buried, wild. And Nietzsche insists: reception as well as creation, the poet and the reader. Any number of writers agree. Blake, on the arts generally: 'Poetry, painting, and music: the three powers of conversing with Paradise which the Flood did not sweep away' (*A Vision of the Last Judgement*). Or Keats, on reading *King Lear*: 'once again, the fierce dispute / Betwixt hell-torment and impassioned clay / Must I burn through'. Engage-ment with art is grappling with articulation at the limits of conscious-ness – intoxication, paradise, hell. And this is not only the view of the Romantic tradition. Ezra Pound invokes Guido Cavalcanti:

> nothing matters but the quality
> of the affection –
> in the end – that has carved the trace in the mind
> dove sta memoria

(Canto LXXVI)

'dove sta memoria': where memory lives. The quality of the affection is finally all that matters – the one thing that makes a poem truly alive to us. T. S. Eliot attends in the same spirit to 'music heard so deeply / That it is not heard at all, but you are the music / While the music lasts' (*Four Quartets*, 'The Dry Salvages'). How can criticism keep in view this fundamental aim of writing and reading – to bring the reader more deeply into contact with what Keats called 'the true voice of feeling'? How can criticism support the quality of affection, the total absorption in the experience of art, that these views imply?

The experience of reading criticism is different from that of engaging with art, but it should be an experience that, because it is designed to deepen that engagement, is not discontinuous with it. Professional criticism, if it has in view bringing the reader into a relationship with a poem that will deepen affection for it, or returning the reader to a work more fully prepared for totally concentrated absorption in it, often has that end in view only very remotely. But writers do envisage criticism in this way. 'You don't really criticise any author to whom you have never surrendered yourself' (T. S. Eliot, in a letter to Stephen Spender, 9 May 1935). Totally absorbed listening has its equivalent in reading: without it the critic can have nothing to say. 'Enthusiastic admiration is the first principle of knowledge and its last' (Blake, contradicting the critical principles of Sir Joshua Reynolds). Knowledge of art does not just begin in enthusiastic admiration: it begins and ends there; enthusiastic admiration is the gamut, the alpha and omega. Wallace Stevens's scepticism about art and intellect points in the same direction:

> They will get it straight one day at the Sorbonne
> We shall return at twilight from the lecture
> Pleased that the irrational is rational,
>
> Until flicked by feeling.
> (*Notes towards a Supreme Fiction*, III.x.)

Feeling will undo the getting-it-straight simplifications of purely rational discourses. Yeats gives a similar view when he admits that engaged reading may require earthbound preliminaries: but the aim is still that the machine aspects of knowledge should be so absorbed into the human as to release us from the study, from the library, for a solitary Yeatsian version of conversation in paradise.

> It is necessary to put so much in order, to clear away so much, to explain so much, that somebody may be moved by a thought or an image that is inexplicable as a wild creature.
>
> ('Samhain: 1902')

Here, criticism and scholarship: there, the effects of beauty on the feelings. They can connect.

Though special knowledge may help the reader to get closer to a poem, and so water the roots of real understanding, it can never stand in place of 'the quality of the affection'. There is an emotional and spiritual vitality which, acting without learning, may by immediate intuition know more of any work of art than learning can ever lead to. Unless this is kept in view, in the kind of activity of mind it implies or promotes, erudition can be – and, more than can be, is – inimical to real knowledge of art. There is a *Dunciad* of modern criticism to be written: Pope's eighteenth-century forms wear historic costumes, but they are eternal types of learned ignorance. So long as art does not affect how we feel, how we think, and so who we are, it is just decoration. If there has been no intoxication, no conversation with paradise, no burning through hell – no effect that is felt through the whole being – then however much criticism may mouth, it can have nothing to say.

* * *

Ways of engaging with art constructed on assumptions quite opposite to this are not only usual in institutional criticism, they are positively promoted – 'interrogating' texts; adopting towards them a stance of detachment; exercising assumptions that contradict the terms of receptivity implied by works themselves; as the torture implication of 'interrogating' implies, analyzing without attention to feeling. Within limits, as one fundamental stance among others, this can be valuable. Participatory enthusiasm without the complement of sceptical critique is the recipe of a Nuremberg rally – a type of phenomenon not confined to Fascism, or even to politics. But with art, when sceptical critique is not a complement to participatory enthusiasm critique has nothing on which to build. There is sometimes a suggestion in professional criticism that establishing an ideological distance between reader and writer can enable critical reflection on the present-day reader's situation – making possible an objective view of the reader's mental world; revealing positive values lost to the ideology from within which we read. But in practice such reflection takes place in one direction only – on the supposed ideological illusions not of the critic but of the writer. Critics regularly imply that, merely as a result of changed historical circumstances, they are morally and politically aware in ways in which the writers who are their subject were not – though typically professional criticism draws on a more limited imaginative experience and a narrower notion of intelligence than that of the writers its detachment patronizes. Scepticism, materialism – whatever the usually inexplicit assumptions of the critic happen to be – are then implicitly presented as Eternal Wisdom.

And while distance and detachment are highly congenial both to etiolated intellectuals and to the scientific knowledge-assumptions of institutions, taken alone sceptical critique is ruinous for participation in aesthetic experience. In any case, art criticism has more than enough of it already. Real understanding of art – like real understanding of religion, or real understanding of people – requires full experience of the complementary polarities: sympathetic engagement; conscious reflection. Before analysis – (I take the word from Susan Sontag) erotics: an intense engagement with the pleasure of the thing itself; a love of surfaces with all your capacity to love, because with art depth is inseparable from surface. Before analysis, and after – and so an analytic mode that makes possible a return to erotics. The complement to analysis, the preliminary to analysis, the final aim of analysis is participation.

Professional criticism is too exclusively concentrated on the intellectual aspects of processes that are not purely intellectual. Even where other kinds of interaction are acknowledged, it does not aim to speak from them, preferring learned procedures the superficial cleverness of which prevents the adept noticing that challenges to articulation are not taking place in the right area, that the kind of analysis encouraged does not engage with the level at which really meaningful interaction – emotional interaction – takes place. Skill in articulation is admired by teachers of literature who are paid to speak and promote speech, but the ability to say something is not necessarily directly related to understanding. Real engagement is often in danger from criticism, which makes the claims of a stimulant for what can be a narcotic, a way in for what is in reality a way round. A Pinteresque script could be written from many a literary-critical discussion which evades real contact with a work by performing around it a dance of questions that predict their own conclusions and so sit happily on the surface of the mind. The apparent communication of perception, where this is a matter of fulfilling a task essentially prescribed by a given framework of thought, can easily be a form of hiding the fact that one is not finding a mode of articulation for what one might really have to say. Language is being used, not as an agent of discovery or instrument of communication, but as a form of shelter, an evasion of puzzlement or incomprehension, recognizing which would be the beginning of a more real understanding. One can often get closer to a work by appropriate silence than by inappropriate verbalizing. Making the tongue wag may keep the spirit dumb.

Proffered techniques for making the tongue wag are legion. The vogue for literary theory epitomizes the problem – a fashion constantly said to be in its death-throes, but continually resuscitated by the vested interests of academic careers and publishing houses, and because the science-based assumptions about knowledge of institutional study require something in the place it occupies – a key or formula that can be presented as systematic and quasi-scientific. The self-conscious study of theories of criticism is one current way of giving literary studies an apparently defining core. In the early institutional study of vernacular literatures, what theory now is, philology was; and subsequently a variety of other programmes were held to give literary studies boundaries and a distinctive character, with some 'stiffening' of quasi-scientific method and intellectual difficulty. But all methodologies should be treated with scepticism. It is characteristic of tools to be toolish. It is characteristic of intellect to become prescriptive and mechanical unless it builds, flexibly and eclectically, on where feeling and imagination lead. For anybody who really finds something of his or her own in a poem, play, or novel, the learned frameworks within which response becomes articulate are continually unravelled by the force of actual experiences struggling to be true to themselves in whatever words they can find. This struggle is not an absolute safeguard against falsity – far from it: articulation can misrepresent experience without being aware of doing so. The struggle for honesty to actual experiences; practice in articulation about a wide range of kinds of work; really digested models of critical thinking; knowledge of the multiplicity of what, beyond the work itself, can be relevant to understanding: these are not absolute safeguards; there are none. But for understanding and deepening what really happens in aesthetic experience, this is the demanding and anarchic recipe. The mixture of life experience and aesthetic experience from which this begins and to which it returns is what is essential.

'Il est trop difficile de penser noblement quand on ne pense que pour vivre' (It is too difficult to think nobly when one only thinks for a living: *Les Confessions*, Book 9, §2). One may stress 'only', or hope that Rousseau's grim verdict admits of exceptions, but still recognize that professional handling will at the least not invariably lead to a heightened liveliness of perception, and that awareness of commentary is perhaps as likely to generate a response that is paralyzingly self-conscious and confused as a response that is deeper and clearer. Consider the situation of the specialist ('expert') in Romantic poetry trying to read freshly (or going through the motions with) the 'Ode on a Grecian Urn'. Might not Keats prefer to think of the poem in the hands of an emotionally imaginative and verbally sensitive teenager, wholly ignorant of the body of commentary his poem has spawned? Certainly anybody engaged in literary studies is familiar with the situation of reading a book or essay from which whatever eager feelings first prompted the writer to engage in some study appear to have been dismally drained.

But independent of the corruptions inherent in professionalization, any deduction from an imagination-thought-feeling complex, by stating that complex in other terms, alters its characteristic modality: intuition becomes self-conscious, the contingent loses conditionality, the exploratory loses tentativeness. These are not small changes. The issue is not only what advanced hierophants of some interpretative method are subtly speculating: it is also – and more prominently – how ordinary believers are wielding the dogmas. With real literary-critical thinking you can never extract templates about method from the texture and language of the thought. As soon as you are in the mode of method, tools, a 'reader's guide', you have radically changed gear. There is a great gulf fixed between a methodology which is a fashionable assumption exercised rigidly, and ideas which result from real experience and are inhabited with a decent tentativeness in recognition of the difficulty of all acts of interpretation; between an eclectic gathering of ideas the intentionally loosely-defined limits of which its holder is always trying imaginatively to evade, and an ideology with well-policed boundaries which is exercised in a spirit of righteous belief.

Sensitivity, honesty, and practice have to interact with a genuinely eclectic investigation of all the ways in which relations with art can be deepened. This is why criticism has to be a subject without boundaries. And unless the interaction keeps in view the desire to deepen passional engagement, that kind of engagement, always difficult, will readily give place to merely outward forms. 'The fascination of what's difficult / Has dried the sap out of my veins': of few people can this be less true than Yeats, but he identifies a central danger posed by the challenge of intellectual difficulty, that it takes over and displaces the desire to understand the complex interaction of aesthetic and life emotions that gave birth to it.

Eclecticism is essential. System is never enough. As the great Romantic poet-novelist-theorist Friedrich Schlegel has it: 'Es ist gleich tödlich für den Geist, ein System zu haben, und keins zu haben. Er wird sich also wohl entschliessen müssen beides zu verbinden'. (*Athenäums-Fragmente*, 53: It is equally fatal for the mind to have a system and to have none. It will just have to decide to combine the two.) Wallace Stevens is yet more radical:

Throw away the lights, the definitions,
And say of what you see in the dark

That it is this or that it is that,
But do not use the rotted names. . . .

Throw the lights away. Nothing must stand

Between you and the shapes you take
When the crust of shape has been destroyed.
(*The Man with the Blue Guitar*, XXXII)

Evangelists of professionalism and self-conscious method, setting the bounds and building the roof, may be eager to deny that it is possible to do what Stevens urges – begin from the beginning; find language freshly responsive to the realities of experience so that experience itself is made new. Whether they or Stevens are better judges of the relation of words to experience their skill with words may attest. People who find themselves keen to deny the possibility of seeing afresh in the creative darkness of finding new words should ask how they know this is not due to their lack of vivid experience and verbal sensitivity.

'I must create a system or be enslaved by another man's.' Blake's spirit of the Imagination utters a cry of creativity at bay needing to establish bases of resistance if it is not to be swamped by forces ranged against it (*Jerusalem*, plate 10). But in practice for Blake this was too simple, or at most a state to be passed through. His fictional Milton is made to see the possibility of founding a new church, and to reject it as inevitably a new cloak for Error. Blake constantly unravelled the systems he created, allowing every aspect of system both to proliferate into gothic complications and to simplify into new symmetries, so that the whole structure is continually in a dynamic state. The complement to Los's wisdom is that we must de-create our own systems or be enslaved by them. If they are not to degenerate into our own clichés we must allow even our own systems to unravel under pressure from the real needs of understanding. 'Make it new' is the slogan Pound devised from the characters on the bathtub of a Chinese emperor: 'cut underbrush, / pile the logs / keep it growing' (Canto LIII). A thoroughly digested sense, worked into the intellectual and emotional bloodstream, of the immense variety of ways in which people have constructed understandings of texts can be of value when really attempting to construct understandings of one's own. But beyond this there can never be a formula. Interpretation is a venture into the unknown without maps – or with many different maps, all potentially but none certainly useful. The methods by which you can establish, investigate, deepen your real relationship with a work are so various, the grounds of choice between them dependent on such a range of issues – about the work and its contexts, the reader and the reader's situation and needs – that you are in effect on your own without a guide.

What is essential is to retain a proper sense of how mysterious understanding art is – how much it can depend on things apparently chance or random, how little it can be formulated into a programme, how much will always be not available to full consciousness, and therefore how foolish are the shibboleths of method and all the confident whistling in the dark that follows from them. Aesthetic experience is a form of wisdom, and no more than wisdom of any other kind is it to be had for the price of obedient adherence to rules.

Criticism is too confident. Its tendency is, though never to say, constantly to imply, that the mode of knowledge it offers – translation into the terms of proposition and argument – is the mode to which art aspires. There the mystifying half statement: the poem. Here the clarified full statement: the criticism. To this vanity of intellect Blake gives the artist's answer.

> Plato has made Socrates say that poets . . . do not know or understand what they write. . . . . This is a most pernicious falsehood. If they do not, pray, is an inferior kind to be called knowing?
>
> ('A Vision of the Last Judgement')

'An inferior kind' – philosophical, of the intellect: inferior to the aesthetic, of the whole person, intellect-feeling-imagination. Many intellectuals are in the position ascribed here to Socrates, that of seeing abstract conceptual thought – their own kind of thought – as the form to which other kinds aspire. Because they do not think in myth, in image, in form, in sound, they think of these – or speak and write as though they think of them – as modes of thought that need translation into the conceptual fully to achieve themselves. But the contrary of this is true: insofar as the meanings embodied in art require the labours of the critic at all, it is for translation into an easier mode of apprehension to give mundane consciousness some purchase by means of which to follow them into their proper sphere.

Vanity of intellect is the obverse of fear of feeling. But in discussing art feeling is vital: finally it is the one essential. Without it whatever can be said, however sophisticated in appearance, is motion without spirit, mechanical, vacuous. Works of art achieve significant life only in the mind of a particular person – reading, seeing, listening. What that reader (viewer, listener) understands a work to mean – because in each person that work is addressing a unique complex of thought and feeling – will inevitably be involved with the experience each brings to the work. Any mode of discussing art that keeps out personal feeling therefore cultivates a central evasion. But although the experiences we bring to reading are always part of our sense of its vital significance, the necessary personal elements in the question 'what does it mean?' – particularly insofar as these are emotional – are regularly shut out by professional criticism. For anyone who sees art as spiritual refreshment keeping the feelings and imagination alive so that ordinary day-to-day levels of experience do not come to seem everything, for anyone for whom it is partly through art that we remain in contact with more fundamental things about life than much day-to-day living provides for, it is essential to bring personal experience into criticism if criticism is to be a worthwhile activity. These fundamental levels of experience that art helps to keep alive, and the values and ideas about life to which they give rise, must be involved. They cannot be if the subjects and modes of criticism are confined to 'interrogation', analysis, and argument.

When I first proposed a form of criticism more overtly engaged with the emotional aspects of art I argued that the precisely personal nature of the critic's engagement should be explicit. As the context of an elaborated reading of Blake I explained the views of religion, politics, sexuality, and literary education that I saw as active in the account of Blake which made up the body of that book (*Blake's Heroic Argument*, 1988). Even as I did this I was uneasy that it gave a mistakenly codified sense of how ideas and values are held and how they interact with reading – that explicit formulation did not register the movements of feeling and thought, but presented the results of those movements as the whole; but the movements of a person's emotional and intellectual life are at least as important as the points at which (always temporarily) they can be caught into stasis. Exposition gives a dogmatic sense of what is provisional, and too rigid a sense of the relation between ideas and experiences. And while one reads from one's experience, part of one's experience is all that one has seriously read. What a properly engaged criticism needs rather is modes and styles that convey more implicitly how perceptions of art arise from experience and feed back into it – modes and styles that enable the whole person to speak, as the conventions of professional criticism do not. One value of writing criticism should be like one value of writing a poem: to deepen and clarify one's feelings, and to make beautiful and expressive verbal structures.

In writing about Shakespeare's Sonnets I have tried to incorporate the interaction between what the reader might bring to and take from reading, keeping to the fore the issue of engaged feeling, by approaching the poems through other works that deal with emotions similar to those expressed in the poems, particularly homosexual feeling in which the beloved acts as a revelation of all that he epitomizes about the world more generally. As William Empson put it in one of a series of love poems to a young man, Desmond Lee, 'You are the map . . . of the divine states / You . . . make known' ('Letter V'). But this kind of experience cannot be summed up in any simple formulation. In Shakespeare's Sonnets the emotions explored range from the most idealistic, in which the beloved is perceived as the epitome of Beauty or Truth, or prompts large-minded reflections about time and death, to an apparent opposite – critical perceptions in which the beloved prompts extreme feelings of bitterness, jealousy, and tortured self-abnegation.

Properly engaged reading both draws on the real perspectives of the reader and recognizes the otherness of the work. It negotiates the Scylla and Charybdis of opposite errors – reading that is too much self-reflection; reading that is too objectified to be emotionally-imaginatively-intellectually real. It means reading that is a full interaction between what is outside oneself to be found and what one brings to the finding. There is a deep difference between postulated possible readings – readings constructed from plausible bits of the interpretations of others; or (as it were) painting-by-numbers, deploying the concepts of some critical method – and vital actual readings – readings true to the feelings, imagination, and ideas of a particular reader. Engaged reading need not be over-partial to the reader's predilections. You should wish to believe that whatever critical account you construct is something that an ideal judge (one might think of it as the author's best self) could recognize as legitimate – an interaction that both respects the otherness of the work and arises from and feeds into the real aesthetic and life experience of the reader.

This book offers two ways of attempting this – engaging with Shakespeare's Sonnets through the kinds of feeling that are fundamental to the young man sequence as these are presented in other kinds of writing and art, from philosophy, poetry, visual art, prose fiction, music, and film; and dwelling in the poems by considering how to read them aloud – reading aloud understood as a mode of interpretation that keeps in the forefront of attention an 'erotics' of the poetry's beautifully meaningful surfaces.

Dwelling in the Feelings

Introduction

'Dwelling in the feelings'. This is an experiment. The idea is, as an adjunct to reading Shakespeare's Sonnets with more emotional engagement, to explore how the love relation central to them, love between an older man (Shakespeare, we may suppose, was about thirty) and a young man (the addressee, we may suppose, was in his late teens), has been explored and understood in other forms of writing and art – in philosophy (Plato), poetry (Michelangelo), visual art (Michelangelo), fiction (Thomas Mann), music (Benjamin Britten), and film (Derek Jarman). My examples are not random, but I have not chosen them for any explicit relation to the Sonnets: I have chosen them for their broad congruence with Shakespeare's poems. In all these forms any number of other works might have been selected – some of which (by Plutarch, Stefan George, Gide) appear on the periphery of the discussions that follow. The idea is through these works to inhabit imaginatively a fundamental emotional area of the Sonnets, and to consider how doing this can help a reader to engage with the Sonnets themselves.

There is no formula for comparison. Congruities of idea or of mode, analogies broad and partial, connections that emerge, often through attention directed to some other end: each affinity is treated on its own terms. The requirements and possibilities are always specific to the work considered. The only method is to use the intelligence, intellectual and emotional. While I have discussed specific congruities of different kinds, the primary aim is more general: it is to inhabit imaginatively an area of feeling with a view to taking the Sonnets themselves with full seriousness as emotional utterances. (Derek Jarman's film is connected to the Sonnets more straightforwardly than the other works considered, but similarly leaves a lot of space for the reader-viewer's interpretative engagement.) The second part of the book – dwelling in the words – is complementary to this. Love of the words in themselves is intensified, I find, by taking seriously their reference to the worlds of experience within and behind the poems. Engagement with the beauty of a poem as a verbal artefact is reinforced by engagement with the experiences it articulates.

The speaker of the Sonnets I shall feel free to call 'Shakespeare', and that is often how I think of the speaker. As with anybody writing in his or her own person, this does not suppose unmediated transcription of experience. It does mean that I imagine for the poems a fundamentally biographical context. Debate about this is as old as Shakespeare criticism itself. Wordsworth and Browning in the nineteenth century, A. C. Bradley and Sir Sidney Lee at the beginning of the twentieth century, took opposite views. Reference to 'the speaker' or 'the persona' of the Sonnets is not an invention of modern criticism. It is as old a position as any other. That it has become the dominant one, and the only one permitted by supposed sophistication, is indicative of the desire of modern criticism to be professional and impersonal. It is an aim dependent on the needs of institutions, not the nature of poetry.

The addressee of the Sonnets I shall call WH, accepting that the dedication of their first publication (the Quarto of 1609) is open to constructions other than that WH (the 'only begetter') is their sole inspiration. I think of WH as HW – Henry Wriothesley, third Earl of Southampton. Southampton is the best traditional candidate for this honour. He is the dedicatee of Shakespeare's two narrative poems (1593, 1594), and the dedication of the second suggests a relationship of greatly increased intimacy within the period usually supposed that in which the Sonnets were largely written, 1592 to 1595. Southampton was beautiful and dashing, and in 1592 he was nineteen. His biographer, Shakespeare's biographer, Park Honan, describes him at twenty-one as having 'the appeal of an androgynous icon' (*Oxford Dictionary of National Biography*). A piece of contemporary gossip suggests that while on military service somewhat later he had a sexual relationship with a fellow officer. That WH was Southampton is conjecture. Other candidates have good claims, and probably the 'lovely' and 'sweet boy' addressed (108, 126) took something from several sweet and lovely boys. Possibly some of them were – as Oscar Wilde proposed (*The Portrait of Mr. W. H.* [Master Willie Hughes]) – lovely boys who played 'Jove's own page', Rosalind-Ganymede, in *As You Like It*, and the other parts Shakespeare wrote for boy-girls with whom men fall in love. My aim is not to affirm some particular historical identity for WH, only to write from the supposition that he had one – or took something from several. I agree with A. C. Bradley that if Shakespeare were inventing a background narrative within which to construct reflections on love he would have constructed a less bizarre framework than that of the Sonnets.

The Sonnets have a background narrative, sometimes somewhat obscurely implied. The first group (1–17), chiding the young man at times for narcissism, urges him ('for love of me', 10.13) to have children so as to preserve his beauty from the depredations of Time. While the argument is that the young man's child (a boy) will be like him, he is like his mother (3): his beauty is feminine. He is also the Platonic idea of truth and beauty (14). These subjects from the first group recur – the poet's love, the youth's feminine beauty, narcissism, Time, the young man as Beauty and Truth. The gap in social status between Shakespeare and the youth, implied in the first group, also becomes a subject (26, 36, 111). Later sonnets intensify the tone of affection: the young man is another self (39, 62, 109), both a cause of emotional turbulence and a support in distress. At first a type of beauty and of congruent moral worth, the youth also begins to appear variously imperfect: by betrayal, behaviour seen as 'sensual' (35) or 'lascivious' (40, 95), mixing in corrupt society (67), shame or 'sport' that appears to be sexual vice (95, 96), and specifically by entering into a relationship with the woman who is the addressee of the last group of poems (40–42, 133–34, 144). Conflicted responses to all this (sometimes within a single sonnet) range from bitter resentment to generous self-abnegation. One sequence (78–86) refers to a poet who rivals Shakespeare for the youth's affection. Faults of Shakespeare's – neglect (100–02) and inconstancy (109, 110) – are complemented by final poems of deep commitment, affirming a love unaffected by Time. The last group of Sonnets (127–54), addressed to a woman traditionally known as the 'Dark Lady', are a parallel and contrast to all this. Here too the love is unconventional: the woman's appearance is an anti-type of Elizabethan beauty; the feeling for her is professedly about sexual compulsion, opposite both to the rarefied (Petrarchan) emotions of Elizabethan sonnet convention, and the spiritualized passions of the WH poems. And as well as being physically unattractive the dark lady is morally reprehensible – a devil to WH's angel (144). In this sequence the lover is named: Will (135, 136).

The nature of the love shown in the Sonnets to WH has prompted as much controversy as almost anything in Shakespeare. As annotators like to point out, 'lover' in the period has a meaning corresponding to the usual modern sense of 'friend' – just as 'friend' in the period has a sense corresponding to the usual modern sense of 'lover' (*OED*, *sb.* 4, from 1490), is used in this sense by Shakespeare (as in *Measure for Measure*, 1.4.29), and colours the tone of address to WH ('fair friend': 104.1). Sense depends on context. 'Lover' does not have its modern meaning in a psalm when paralleled to 'friend' (Bishops' Bible [1568], 38.11), but in the context of 'and there reigns Love and all Love's loving parts' (31) it is nonsense to claim that a use in the psalter shows the word was regularly stripped of its modern erotic sense – which Shakespeare also used (as in *Measure for Measure*, 1.4.39). Similarly 'spend' (ejaculate: 4.1), 'traffic' (sexual commerce: 4.9), 'treasure' (semen: 6.4), 'passion' (physical sexual desire, 20.2), 'mistress' (in 'master mistress', a man loved like a woman, 20.2): it may be that none of these words necessarily carry the sexual senses that were available in the period; it is a matter of judgement whether they are activated by context. But recognizing that the Sonnets to WH reflect feelings commonly involved in erotic relationships (whether or not thought of as consummated) does not depend on accepting verbal nuances that can be judged more or less probable in relation to an uncertain linguistic community – WH, friends among whom manuscript copies were reportedly circulated, purchasers of the 1609 Quarto, lovers of all times and places ('all posterity / That wear this world out to the ending doom'). It depends on a view of the quality of feeling the poems exhibit: the intensity of what is plainly called – again and again – 'love', and sometimes 'desire'; the all-but-overwhelmed response to the wonder of the sweet and lovely boy's beauty; the horror at its transience as epitomizing all depredations of time; the pains and fears of absence, jealousy, betrayal, and obsession, which cause bitter distress, insomnia, and self-abasement; the penitence expressed for ingratitude and unfaithfulness. If these are not feelings commonly involved in erotic relationships, I have no judgement in love.

'Boy' in what follows means, as in Germaine Greer's *The Boy* (2003), a youth or young man between the ages of about sixteen and twenty-four. As Germaine Greer argues, to some extent biologically, and even more culturally, youth is variable and constructed. In what follows when 'boy' refers to a youth under sixteen that is made clear. Though Greer argues or assumes that the art she discusses usually presupposes a (female) heterosexual viewer, her interest in reclaiming subversive forms of love is broadly just as amenable to (male) homosexual feeling. Her examples and discussions offer copious alternatives for dwelling in the feelings through painting and sculpture to the examples from Michelangelo discussed here.

My experiment raises the issue of how I envisage the reader. Most readers of literary criticism are in effect professionals, reading in an institutional context with a productive purpose shaped by that context – the purpose of producing more discourse: undergraduate essay, postgraduate thesis, academic lecture, article or critical book. But suppose a reader whose aim is not conditioned by these purposes, whose aim is unproductive poetic pleasure, and who hopes to emerge from this pleasure with the imagination enlarged and even – recognizing that this happens more rarely – with the sensibility modified. Such a reader might be happy to accept the accounts in what follows of Plato, Michelangelo, Mann, Britten, and Jarman; and I have accordingly tried to convey the flavour of the works I discuss as well as the issues. But ideal readers may well turn aside to read, look, and listen for themselves. Where the aim is aesthetic pleasure and engaged sensibility, why not?

> I just as much as my book, are friends of *lento*. It is not for nothing that I have been a philologist, perhaps I am a philologist still, that is to say, a teacher of slow reading. . . . Nowadays it is not only my habit, it is also my taste – a malicious taste perhaps? – no longer to write anything which does not reduce to despair every sort of man who is 'in a hurry'. For philology is that venerable art which demands of its votaries one thing above all: to go aside, to take time, to become still, to become slow – it is a goldsmith's art and connoisseurship of the *word* which has nothing but delicate, cautious work to do and achieves nothing if it does not achieve it *lento*. But for precisely this reason it is more necessary than ever today, by precisely this means does it entice and enchant us the most, in the midst of an age of 'work', that is to say, of hurry, of indecent and perspiring haste, which wants to 'get everything done' at once, including every old or new book: – this art does not so easily get anything done, it teaches to read *well*, that is to say, to read slowly, deeply, looking cautiously before and aft, with reservations, with doors left open, with delicate eyes and fingers. (Nietzsche, *Daybreak: Thoughts on the Prejudices of Morality*, Preface, §5)

Of course few can hope to offer the reader who learns not to hurry so much as this teasing philosopher. But Nietzsche's point is not only about how to read him: it is about how to read anything in a way that is worthwhile. If what one reads cannot justify this lover of the word's desire for *lento* – 'to go aside, to take time, to become still' – then one should read something else. In this sense, poetry always requires philology; and for this the utilitarian attitudes implicit in institutional critical reading regularly have about them too little of going aside, taking time, or becoming still. My aim is to convey enough of Plato, Michelangelo, Mann, Britten, and Jarman for these accounts to work of themselves as ways of dwelling in the feelings; and to embody these prelusory engagements fully and vividly, recognizing that, as they have to be to match Shakespeare's poetry, the works themselves are highly sophisticated: their exposition requires elaboration. The readings are, of course, my own. Undoubtedly my accounts will work better if they are prefaces to the reader's own reading, looking, and listening.

Plato, *Symposium* and *Phaedrus*

Plato asks the fundamental questions. What is love? And what is the role in love of the erotic? Is love an end in itself? Or is the response to beauty of outward form or inward being that we call love an intimation of forces that transcend what first prompts them? In Plato, discussion of these issues centres on homosexual love, which in classical Greek culture was a normal aspect of male sexuality. (The standard account, with detailed exemplification from law, literature, and visual art, is K. J. Dover, *Greek Homosexuality*.) Modern sexual identities, which understand homosexuality as a predisposition within a minority of individuals, on the Greek view can be seen as still grounding their assumptions in the ban Christianity derived from Judaism. On this view, while the ban has been overturned, its fundamental effect remains in place. The illegitimate is legitimated; for most men norms of feeling remain as they were. What is unusual in Shakespeare's Sonnets, in his culture and in ours, in a Greek, and specifically in a Platonic context, may appear attuned to a more comprehensive sense of possibility in love between men.

In Plato, Love is a fundamental and universal force, directing all activity in the human, natural, and celestial worlds. Love of beauty is the root of, and the route to, *philosophia*, love of wisdom. But not all loves lead to wisdom. In *Symposium* speakers distinguish between radically different forms of human love. Love governed by common Aphrodite is concerned with sex above everything else; it is directed towards men or women. Love governed by heavenly Aphrodite is concerned with the whole being – beauty, intelligence, and moral worth; it is directed exclusively towards men. Heavenly Aphrodite does not forbid sex, provided sex expresses appreciation of the beloved's whole nature. This is expressed at the drinking party ('symposium' gives a misleading idea of sobriety) by Pausanius, but in Xenophon's *Symposium* (§8) the same distinction is made by the more authoritative Socrates. Pausanius endorses the noble homosexuality encouraged by heavenly Aphrodite by contrasts: contrast with Sparta – bad because its military ethos encourages purely physical homosexuality; contrast with Persia – bad because its tyranny discourages all homosexuality as a form of love which, by creating bonds between men who love freedom, is associated with resistance to tyrants. 'Love's not Time's fool' (116): to be noble, love, which begins as a response to beauty, must be drawn ultimately to what survives change – not physical beauty, but intellectual and moral worth. But physical beauty and physical expression have a place in love. And the noblest form of love is, as in the Shakespeare Sonnets, that between an older man and a younger: there most that is of value can be bestowed – the love of knowledge, and principles of wisdom and virtue. Ideally the younger man should be on the verge between youth and early manhood: then beauty is most intense, and openness to intellectual and moral instruction most acute.

There are other points of view in the dialogue, and there are non-discursive ways of expressing ideas, particularly a myth devised by Aristophanes of two-part separated but once complete beings whose fundamental desire is for reunion with their other half. Comic as it is in Aristophanes' telling, this myth has the serious aim of recognizing that Love has semi-inexpressible aspects: desire for complete (and impossible) union with the beloved (as in Sonnets 22, 36, 109); desire for complete wholeness of one's own being, which only 'the marriage of true minds' (116) can bring fully into existence.

Given that Plato's discourse does not work by rational progression it cannot be interpreted only in terms of its arguments. Socrates is established as a powerful character before the party begins, and his ironic wit establishes his authority in the immediate situation. But Socrates's irony mainly applies to (and undermines) the sophistic 'eloquence' of Agathon. It does not invalidate the myth of Aristophanes or the arguments of Pausanius. So even when Socrates presents the source of his wisdom, Diotima, the reader is not given the voice of a final arbiter. Diotima is an itinerant charismatic seer: her mode is distinctively non-Socratic. While she begins by using Socratic question-and-answer, increasingly she turns to myth-making, intuitive extrapolation, and rhapsodic assertion. Diotima is an *alter ego*, the Wisdom of Socrates, but she is wisdom in an unusual form. In presenting his wisdom as female Socrates presents himself, Tiresias-like, as trans-gendered. As in Plato's *Theaetetus*, where Socrates is a mid-wife helping men and boys to bring ideas into being (149a–151c), in the sexual imagery of Diotima's account the philosopher's spiritual and mental pregnancy gives birth to virtuous actions, creations, or teachings. The apparent paradox about mysteries of man-boy love being articulated by a female voice, and in terms of giving birth, recognizes that even in ancient Greek society, this love was seen as potentially and even dangerously fluid in gender.

Diotima's fundamental idea is that professed mysteries of love show that a central motivating force of life is the desire for immortality, the 'war with time' (15) of the Sonnets. At a lower level of development (animals, ordinary human beings, heterosexuals) this immortality is physical – through children: sex, when not simply sensual pleasure, is for procreation. But at a higher level the immortality to which life aspires is spiritual – through the creation of civil society, philosophy, poetry: superior to physical begetting, homosexual, the final finest fruit of loving boys – though its ultimate aim (in Plato, not in Shakespeare) is to leave behind its basis in response to an individual. The ideal has been criticized as egotistical, for treating the beloved instrumentally, as a passing phase in the lover's spiritual progress. Insofar as he acts on the ideal of Diotima, the effect Socrates produces is to reverse the usual emotional dynamic by which the *erastes* (lover) pursues and the *eromenos* (beloved) is pursued. While the obvious analogy for Shakespeare in this is the older and power-fully creative Socrates, there is also a sense therefore in which Socrates is like WH. By being 'unmoved, cold' and to temptation more than slow, utterly resistant (Sonnet 94), Socrates creates an obsession in his pupils that reverses the usual emotional dynamic and produces a dependency of which they are at times – like the speaker of the Sonnets – resentful. Shakespeare writes from both extremes of the Platonic gam-ut. While love is key to a sense of life that goes quite beyond the relationship with one individual, as in the many sonnets that incorporate general meditations on love or on time, the sonnets, particularly towards the end of the 'lovely boy' sequence (116, 123–25), that affirm eternity in love ('even to the edge of doom'), make clear that this love does not leave behind the relationship with the individual. WH is and remains the particular beloved whose idiosyncratic behaviours cause specific joys and sufferings. Like the beloved in Plato, he also epitomizes love as a cosmic force. The arche-typal beautiful youth, Adonis, and the archetypal beautiful woman, Helen (53), the comprehensive 'master-mistress' (20), he sums up Socrates' aim in philosophy, through Beauty to reach Truth (14, 54, 101). Particular beauties are 'but figures of delight / Drawn after' WH: he is the 'pattern' for all of them (98).

Diotima's account of Love is more profound than those that pre-cede it, and presentation by Socrates gives it a different status; but the noisy, drunken, and comic intrusion of Alcibiades means that, even in *Symposium*, it is far from a last word. Alcibiades – once the perfec-tion of boy-beauty, as Socrates affirms in *Protagoras* (309a) – rein-states the competition of more or less resonant voices. Though he offers testimony to Socrates' chastity, he also shows that Socrates' charisma is not based on the dispassionate love of moral and intellectual beauty prescribed by Diotima. Quite the reverse: the intensity of Socrates' discourse draws from the immediate inspiration of beautiful young men – in the past, Alcibiades; at the party, Agathon. Like WH, the beautiful youth is a Muse. (That Socrates had powerful desires to restrain is humorously illustrated in *Charmides* (155c–156d), when catching sight of the youthful body of Charmides underneath his tunic causes Socrates the most passionate confusion ('I was on fire! I was in ecstasy!'). Overcome by his glimpse of boy-beauty, he is comically unable to speak when the lovely youth addresses him, and regains composure only by a disquisition on temperance. Evidently transcending this intensity of response required all the heroic self-control to which Alcibiades testifies.)

In making sense of the multiplicity of voices in *Symposium* there may be a clash of more or less philosophical and literary ways of reading. Philosophical: there is finally truth; the purpose of interpretation is to elicit truth. Literary: different truths are embedded in an undecidable contest of perspectives; the purpose of interpretation is to elicit embeddedness, context, and relationships. *Symposium* is as much literary as philosophical: undecidability is implicit in its mode. Socrates is a character in a historical fiction: his way of approaching truth is different from that of the fiction that gives him his existence. Even his speech introducing Diotima is situated: he begins from a response to the beautiful young man it is his pleasure to tease, Agathon. And the whole set of reported arguments, myths and comic stories is given an elaborate fictional frame – a report (incomplete) of a report (faulty) of an occasion years earlier, which included contributions professedly forgotten, at which most of the speakers were recovering from a bout of heavy drinking the previous day. Because of the authority Socrates accords Diotima, and because Alcibiades was not able to seduce Socrates, what was extrapolated from this riot of points of view became known as 'Platonic love' – love without sex. But this is quite different from what resonates most out of the drinking-party's imbroglio of reasoned, rhapsodic, mythic, and comic embodiments, which has much more of the variousness about love of the Sonnets.

Extrapolation from Plato of a dominant idea of love is even more problematic if *Symposium* is set beside *Phaedrus*. In *Phaedrus* Socrates affirms the value of extreme states of consciousness, of inspiration over technique, and generally of the extraordinary over the ordinary; and he distinguishes between divine madness and dull sanity in religion, in poetry, and in love. The 'madness' of love is especially highly valued because, correctly contemplated, the beauty of the beloved – physical, intellectual, and moral – is the key to understanding true being. The lover experiences through the beloved awe, reverence, and intense longing: described as a painful growth of the soul's 'wings', this longing images the transcendence of self inspired by love. As in the Sonnets that treat love as in some sense religious (105, 106, 108), Love is set by Plato in the broadest possible context, of understanding the soul and the soul's place in the universe.

This view of love is different from that of *Symposium*. In *Phaedrus* Socrates depicts the soul as tripartite, a charioteer guiding two horses, one good, one bad. The charioteer can be understood primarily as reason, and the two horses primarily as the appetitive and spiritual aspects of being – but this is myth not allegory: in both horses *eros* may be present, and all three aspects of the soul partake of qualities of each other. The expression of physical desire should be governed by reason, but even the most exalted kind of love does not, as in Diotima's account, leave behind the beloved or the erotic. Both horses may be involved so long as the bad horse does not get out of control. At the climax of Socrates's mythical hymn celebrating Love, one of the most impassioned and professedly 'inspired' statements in all Plato's writings, addressed to the god of love and prompted by the 'beautiful boy' Phaedrus (252b) – after a passionate account of the pains of unsatisfied longing, and the promptings to god-like being of reciprocated love – the union of minds through bodies, physical expression prompted by reciprocal recognition of intellectual beauty, is approved. Physical love-making is the proper deepening of a sacred relation on an only slightly lower plane – for heroic rather than philosophical types. This could scarcely be more exalted, and it is distinctly different from Diotima's ethic in *Symposium*. In *Phaedrus* the method is not principally question-and-answer – 'Socratic'; the ideal of love is not insistently non-physical – 'Platonic'.

The different implications of *Symposium* and *Phaedrus* are parallel to different ways of reading the WH Sonnets overall, as about an undoubtedly passionate but finally (in the conventional sense) 'Platonic' love, or as about a love that is both passionate and erotic. 'A woman's face with nature's own hand painted' (20), has sometimes been taken to resolve doubts about this, but witty readers have seen more in its lewd resolution than suits a determined heterosexism.[1] As often, a long-running disagreement in the history of criticism implies that its oppositions are both true. WH is the focus of the Platonic spectrum: passionate desire and quasi-religious reverence.

(The fundamental issue here is not influence but congruence. But insofar as Shakespeare understood love in terms actually filtered from Plato, it may be relevant that Plato was thought of in the Renaissance as having a licentious side because of the homosexual loves and poems attributed to him in Diogenes Laertius' *Lives of the Philosophers* [III.29–33], mostly famously, 'Kissing Agathon, my soul leapt to my lips, as if eager, poor wretch, to pass over to him'; and, among his lovers, the boy, Aster [Star]).

Its view of Love apart, *Phaedrus* also presents an objection to writing which is precisely the objection to literary criticism composed purely in the intellect, not on the fundamental basis of the intellect interpreting and giving form to the feelings. Whether or not the arguments of Socrates constitute an objection to written discourse *per se*, or an objection to all-too-usual degenerate forms of writing, Plato, who wrote this diatribe against writing, can scarcely have thought of it as more than a partial truth. (Derrida ['Plato's Pharmacy' (1968), *Disseminations*, 1972, 1981], presents it as a classic instance of discourse that unthreads its ostensible aims by contradictions built into its expression.) But however one reads it, there is a real problem: words must be 'truly written in the soul' (276a, 278a). Socrates' arguments are directed not only at writing but also at reading. The problem for readers is to receive words so as to connect them fully with the realities of which they are symbols. *Symposium*'s appeals to the feelings and imagination as well as the intellect address this difficulty implicitly. *Phaedrus* revises *Symposium* so as to make fully explicit the difficulties of engaging the reader's whole being in acts of reading.

The narrative and dramatic nature of the texts, the presentation of characters who discover and explore meaning through dialogue, the address to feeling and imagination by myth and symbol as well as to the intellect with logic and argument, mean that these dialogues are peculiarly open to the various and interactive engagement that leads to words being 'written on the soul of the hearer'. Their multiplicity also means that they are particularly open to variety of interpretation. Both dialogues are steeped in boy-love, and finally the point is not what Socrates decides should be done with Eros, but that for Socrates philosophizing is an erotic activity. As in the Sonnets, the Beauty that leads to Truth begins from – and in the *Phaedrus* account may be permanently supported by – the love of a boy.

Michelangelo, Poems and Drawings

Unlike with Shakespeare, we know to whom Michelangelo's poems were written and a considerable amount about their biographical circumstances. Some forty poems were addressed to 'the young Tommaso dei Cavalieri', who, as Giorgio Vasari put it in a biography that Michelangelo approved, Michelangelo loved 'infinitely more than any'. 'Matchless and unequalled – light of our century, paragon of the world': so Michelangelo addressed Tommaso, in what was perhaps his first attempt at a letter to him. And, feeling the inadequacy of words ('read the heart and not the letter'), he quoted Petrarch (canzone 23): 'affection exceeds the compass of the pen' (draft letter of 1 January 1533). A few months later, when Tommaso apparently complained that Michelangelo's feeling for him had slackened, the artist responded: 'I could as soon forget your name as forget the food on which I live . . . I am insensible to sorrow or fear of death, while my memory of you endures' (letter of 28 July 1533). 'So are you to my thoughts as food to life' (75).

Michelangelo met Tommaso in 1532, when Michelangelo was fifty-seven. The 'young' Tommaso's age is not known, but it is now generally accepted that he was indeed young – perhaps sixteen or seventeen (Zöllner), perhaps twelve or thirteen (Panofsky-Soergel). As with Shakespeare and WH, there was also a gap of social status: the Cavalieri were from the Roman ruling elite. Nevertheless, Tommaso remained one of Michelangelo's closest friends throughout his life, and was with him when he died in 1564. From their first meeting Michelangelo seems to have been seized by feelings for Tommaso of an intensity unprecedented in his experience, feelings he found all but overwhelming, which he expressed in poems, letters, and drawings. Though Michelangelo later considered (and abandoned) a plan to publish some of the poems, they were written as part of a private dialogue. Like the Shakespeare Sonnets, they sometimes refer to circumstances not entirely explicable without knowledge exclusive to the writer and addressee, so that both sets of poems have at times the character and intimacy of overheard private conversation.

Understanding how Michelangelo grappled with and formulated the feelings he expresses in the poems requires at one level nothing but careful reading. Like some of his sculptures, many are rugged, fragmentary constructions which, with a minimum of typically Renaissance rhetorical shaping, speak with almost naked simplicity. But utterance could not always be direct. Like Shakespeare, Michelangelo worked in a context where boys (as models) took the roles of women – an environment, which as a result was (like the Elizabethan theatre) regularly accused of encouraging homosexuality. He recognized that his feelings for Tommaso might be seen as, and in the terms of his Christian culture and his own beliefs might even be, sinful. The care taken by contemporary biographers to rebut any suggestion of earthly passion in Michelangelo's delight in male beauty; Michelangelo's comments on vulgar misunderstanding of his feelings (poems 58, 83); the complaint of Pietro Aretino that only 'Gherardi e Tomai' could obtain drawings from Michelangelo (Gherardo Perini: a man Michelangelo knew from the early 1520s); the publication of the poems by his great-nephew (1623) in which the male pronouns were silently changed: all these indicate how Michelangelo's friendships with young men might be perceived by contemporaries. Michelangelo's ways of understanding and formulating his emotions were, in response to this, influenced – as were Shakespeare's – by Plato and by Petrarch.

Michelangelo grew up in the Florence of the great Renaissance Platonist, Marsilio Ficino. Ficino wrote about love in terms derived from the *Symposium* and the *Phaedrus*, and he did so in a context – regulated by Christian assumptions – that put those ideas into practice. Ficino wrote love-letters (published in his lifetime) to a younger man, Giovanni Cavalcanti, to whom he dedicated his commentary on the *Symposium*, and with whom he lived. That his translations of and commentaries on Plato led to an exalted and sexually charged view of male friendship is clear. It is open to question how far he was central to a society in which loving friendships between men took forms we would now recognize as homosexual. Certainly the knowledge of Platonic writings on love reflected in Michelangelo's poems arose from a context of more than purely scholarly interpretation and application.

The other important influence on how Michelangelo expressed his feelings for Tommaso was Petrarch. The love poems addressed by Petrarch to a woman he called Laura affected how poets wrote about love for three centuries. Shakespeare is still responding to them several decades after Michelangelo. Laura was an actual woman, but not a focus of erotic feeling that could be consummated: the probable historical Laura was already married when Petrarch first saw her in 1327. Non-consummation is built into the situation assumed in the poems to her, and principal elements of the experience, particularly moral pressure to deflect physical desire, therefore readily transfer to homosexual love in the Christian culture of Michelangelo. Michelangelo could use Petrarchan conventions, not because they were accepted terms of love poetry, but because the experiences that gave rise to them were congruent with his own. As his contemporary Francesco Berni put it, '[Petrarchists] say words, Michelangelo says things'.

Michelangelo's poems to Tommaso give expression to feelings that, whatever their philosophical and religious complexities, had some erotic content that could not usually be expressed erotically. The poems often treat the role of the senses, desire, an all-but-overwhelmed response to Tommaso's physical beauty, seeing these sometimes as positive preliminaries to spiritual love, sometimes as potential barriers. The basic positions that Michelangelo struggles to sustain are a Christian vision of human beauty as a divine creation, to be contemplated as an intimation of the divine nature, and a Neo-Platonic vision of love leading through and beyond the individual to the eternal.

'Se l'immortal desio' (58: If desire of the immortal) is an index of central issues: the difficulty of understanding love; that it cannot be wholly manifested or understood through the senses. Those who interpret love such as his as carnal desire (Michelangelo argues) show only their own corruption. Properly understood, love is a desire for what is immortal: love contains intimations of a vision of God. There is a concern with carnal 'misunderstanding'. Expression, and on occasion what is expressed, show that this concern does not come only from outside. It is forced on Michelangelo by his experience: the senses and desire insistently assert their validity against ideas that seek to contain or negate them.

'S'un casto amor' (59: If one chaste love) is typical of poems in which love is viewed as raising the lovers towards the divine. Michelangelo identifies the lovers with each other totally: as in many of Shakespeare's sonnets, their 'undivided loves are one' (36), 'un'anima in duo corpi' (one soul in two bodies). Like Zeus and

Ganymede, they rise to heaven 'con pari ale' (with the same wings). But expression is not entirely congruent with the affirmation of chaste feeling. 'Amor' with his golden arrow, 'le viscer . . . arda' (burns the bowels) – a bodily effect, suggesting a bodily cause. Syntax repeatedly strains towards but is deflected from completion – 'if . . . if . . . if' (ten times 'if'): it is the melancholy music of unfulfilled yearning. Holy thought struggles with passionate feeling.

Some poems are straightforwardly Neo-Platonic: love of human beauty raises the soul to knowledge of the divine. The same fundamental idea is expressed with many variations. Love is not about desire, the senses, the perishing body: it is the immortal soul – of which external beauty is evidence – that prompts love. Ultimately human beauty is a vision of God:

> . . . Dio, suo grazia, mi si mostra altrove
> più che 'n alcun leggiadro e mortal velo;
> e quel sol amo perch'in lui si specchia.

(106.12–14)

(God, in his graciousness, does not show himself more fully to me elsewhere than in some lovely, mortal veil; and I love that solely because in it He is reflected.)

The effect of Tommaso's beauty is like Beatrice's for Dante – an analogy specifically implied in 'I' mi credetti' (80). That another poem in its final form addressed to Tommaso (81) was first drafted with female pronouns implies that – while he would have repudiated with holy horror Shakespeare's Caravaggesque 'master mistress' – Michelangelo recognized in his feelings for Tommaso something trans-gendered.

But even where love is viewed simply as holy it can be problematic. 'Non so se s'è la desïata luce' (76: I do not know if it is the longed-for light) entertains a religious view of love, but also searches speculatively for other explanations for love's intensity, admitting that recognized accounts are not adequate to experience. Michelangelo can tell the immediate source – 'certo saranno stati gli occhi vostri' (it is certainly your eyes that have brought this about) – but he can only wonder about fundamental causes. 'I' mi son caro' (90: I am much dearer to myself) is exultant: Michelangelo's feelings for Tommaso give him a sense of almost God-like powers – the ability to perform miracles analogous to those of Christ. The exuberant claims can be given a naturalistic sense: the artist cures blindness by showing people how to see; the artist cures poisoning by redirecting distorted emotional and imaginative faculties. But the images by which inspiration derived from Tommaso is conveyed mingle secular and sacred love astoundingly – and heretically: the extreme Protestant Family of Love might believe that we all have in us an element of Christ, but the Catholic and Apostolic Church of Rome did not. 'Spargendo il senso il troppo ardor cocente' (93: When the senses spread their excessive, searing heat) presents love for Tommaso (finally) as holy, an agreement between the senses, heart, soul, and reason. But before the pious conclusion, the interest is in the heart 'che del più ardente / foco più vive' (which draws most life from the most fiercely burning fire). Agreement of the faculties is not settled without a struggle. The heart may be seen by the soul as wrong, but this is not a simple error: it is part of Love positively valued for producing greater intensity of being. Similarly 'Al cor di zolfo' (97: If one's heart is made of sulphur): Michelangelo's feeling for Tommaso is a destiny over which, because of his passionate sensitivity to beauty, he cannot exercise control. Though he acknowledges that this results from personal failings (weakness of reason; lack of emotional restraint), he ultimately blames the nature of his being – and hence (explicitly) the Creator. As in so many poems, Michelangelo really puzzles about the nature of his love, and whether it should be viewed negatively or positively – here as a manifestation of the sensitivity to beauty fundamental to his ability as an artist.

And while all but the most positive poems contain undercurrents of doubt and pain, some go further. Even when beauty is an intimation of the divine, its effects can be other than elevating. 'Dal dolce pianto al doloroso riso' (78: From sweet lament to suffering smile) admits that in response to Tommaso's beauty the sensual may predominate, and that this may come to seem not unwelcome. 'Quantunche 'l tempo ne constringa e sproni' (92: Although time forces us and spurs us) goes further. Love is morally dubious, Michelangelo's habitual error ('error consueto'): far from being a proper response to beauty as a revelation of the divine, love here deflects from the divine goal. 'Crudele stella' (70: Cruel star) presents Michelangelo's passions as repeating the sin of Adam and Eve and as depriving him of heaven. When not conceived as the Platonic ladder, love could be the road to Hell. 'Se nel volto per gli occhi il cor si vede' (72: Since a person's heart is seen in his face through his eyes) shows why. There is a passionately physical aspect to his love for Tommaso, a desire to hold 'il desïato mie dolce signore / per sempre nell'indegne e pronte braccia' (my sweet, longed-for lord forever in my unworthy and yet ready arms). This is the most direct expression of physical yearning in the poems to Tommaso, but it makes explicit what is implicit elsewhere. And a draft expressed yet more specifically the desire to embrace 'il petto e 'l collo al mie signore' (the breast and neck of my lord). Even before this striking conclusion Michelangelo conflates heavenly and earthly passion. Since he cannot deserve Tommaso's love through merit, an expression of love for him by Tommaso would be congruent with the operation of God's grace. This is neither Christian nor Neo-Platonic, and the idea that Time might stop at such a moment recalls not only – and blasphemously – the Last Judgement but also classical erotic poetry.

It suggests another perspective on these struggles that Tommaso was not the only youth about whom Michelangelo wrote poems. Two poems addressed to or about Febo di Poggio (99, 100), with whom Michelangelo had some emotional and perhaps sexual relationship not long after he met Tommaso, and to whom he referred as a 'little blackmailer', indicate that Michelangelo was not only sensitive to beauty that could be construed as intellectual and spiritual. And in response to a request from his friend Luigi del Riccio, Michelangelo also wrote a series of fifty epitaphs on the death of del Riccio's cousin, Cecchino (Francesco) Bracci. The degree of Michelangelo's engagement in writing these poems is uncertain. He first met Cecchino in 1542, two years before the boy's death at the age of fifteen. References to Cecchino in his letters are admiring and affectionate. An acute problem is raised by one poem, 'La carne terra' (197: My flesh, being earth – supposed as spoken by Cecchino). For this Michelangelo provided an alternative ending about embracing Cecchino in bed. Quite what the lines mean has been a subject of controversy. But if the nature of Michelangelo's engagement with Cecchino is uncertain, his engagement with Febo is clear: he found him attractive, and not because he raised his soul to heaven.

As well as writing poems to Tommaso dei Cavalieri Michelangelo gave him a number of highly finished drawings. Michelangelo described these in a sonnet to Tommaso as 'turpissime' (79, of the basest kind) – a comment that can be taken either as a modest estimate of their artistic quality or as a hint about their sexual implications. They are in part forms of reassurance, recognizing the dangers of illicit or unregulated passion. They also appear to be forms of covert confession – acknowledgements that the passions they depict might be seen in different ways.

Archers shooting at a Herm (Zöllner, plate 204) Goethe seems broadly right to understand as depicting 'the power of the fleshly lusts' (*Reisejournal*, 14 March 1788). Michelangelo probably intended the image to be understood as allegorical: the herm-soul is protected by the shield of divine grace or an enlightened (Neo-Platonic) understanding of the relation of physical to intellectual beauty; the young men (including Michelangelesque types of ideal grace and loveliness) are instigators of desire; their bows and arrows (invisible, metaphorical) represent forms in actual life of the mythical Eros who sleeps below them. Tommaso is reassured: though passion's sources are vehicles of powerful energy, they can be kept at bay.

The Fall of Phaëton (Zöllner, plates 197–99) has a similar implication. The drawing shows the disastrous end of Phaëton's hubristic attempt to drive the chariot of the sun. Above, Zeus, mounted on his eagle, stops him with a thunderbolt; Phaëton and the chariot with its four horses plunges down; below, Phaëton's sisters, the Heliades, look on in horror. The image exemplifies aspiration beyond what is permitted to the human – transgressive desire, and the suffering that follows from violating divine fiat. Classical myths were often read as implying Christian meanings *avant la lettre*: Ovid's account (*Metamorphoses*, II. 304–400), comparing Phaëton to a falling star, in a Christian context suggests the fall of Lucifer/Satan. The drawing has a Christian meaning of general application about the sin of Pride. But Tommaso could also read it as having a specific meaning: Michelangelo understands that his aspirations may be congruent with those of Phaëton; he must avoid the suffering and chaos created by illicit desire.

Two other drawings given to Tommaso are open to interpretations less reassuringly holy. *The Rape of Ganymede* (Zöllner, plate 257) shows the Idean shepherd boy seized by Zeus in the form of an eagle. The god-bird grasps the boy's legs with his feet and claws and, with the boy's arms resting on his outstretched wings, flies up with him into the heavens. The myth had a standard Neo-Platonic interpretation: love inspires spiritual ascent. But the myth could not but be recognized as also a narrative of homoerotic violence: the eagle in Michelangelo's drawing can scarcely be seen as other than expressing carnal desire; the boy – in his swooning passivity – is at least not resisting the bird's embrace. As an image of spiritual ascent this looks very physical. Given that the source is a narrative of rape (Ovid, *Metamorphoses*, 10.155–65), the posture of the fiercely gripping predatory eagle-god might suggest to all but the most chaste viewer the possibility of anal penetration. A meaning compatible with Christian morality and reassuring to Tommaso, consistent with the less tortured of Michelangelo's poems, can be imposed – but what the image shows when not viewed through Christian or Neo-Platonic filtering is passionate desire and permissive response.

Michelangelo perhaps felt that this scarcely veiled release of passion required a complement, which is what the companion drawing, *The Punishment of Tityos*, ostensibly provides (Zöllner, plate 203). Tityos was a Titan who attempted to rape Leto, the mother of Apollo and Artemis. For this he was cast into hell, where a vulture feeds perpetually on his liver (seat of the passions). Michelangelo could have known the myth from several sources, but most relevant is Lucretius, *De rerum natura* (3.984–94), in which Tityos is interpreted as symbolic of a man for whom love means being 'devoured by agonizing anguish'. And Tityos does not only suffer for sexual sin: in Dante (*Inferno*, 31) he is in the lowest circle of Hell with other Titans who rebelled against Zeus. Sexual sin leads to defection from God. The drawing forms a pair with the *Ganymede*: they are visually as well as ideologically complementary, so much so that the bird in *Tityos* (a vulture in the myth) closely resembles the *Ganymede* eagle. A Neo-Platonic reading of *Ganymede* complements the plain sense of *Tityos*: spiritual love leads to heaven, carnal love to hell. The two figures are assailed by passion (the same violent bird) with contrasting effects. But like *Ganymede*, *Tityos* is open to a less pious reading. The Titan is a beautiful and heroic figure; his chains are ribbons; his attitude does not express resistance or pain; there are no exposed viscera for the divinely-commissioned vulture-eagle to tear. Scarcely less than Ganymede does this victim surrender to the bird's domination. Both drawings leave open implications congruent with the forbidden desires that disrupt the Neo-Platonism of Michelangelo's poems.

Michelangelo's holy-profane struggles were not Shakespeare's, but the Sonnets do treat love as sacred. 'Religious love' prompts 'holy . . . tear[s]' (31); Love is 'consecrate' to WH (74); he belongs to a world 'holy' in its authenticity (68); thoughts directed to him 'intend a zealous pilgrimage' (27); to mention his name freely would be 'profane' (89). The Sonnets are like prayers (108) – even (blasphemously) like the Lord's Prayer ('hallowed thy . . . name'). 'Let not my love be called idolatry' (105) – but the disclaimer presents WH's comprehensive trio of virtues in terms that imitate the Trinitarian rhetoric of the Athanasian Creed. In this context the youth by whom 'all losses are restored and sorrows end' (30) is Christ-like. Whereas Michelangelo connects his experience of love with a total system of thought in which religion is primary, in the Sonnets, as in the companion poem *A Lover's Complaint*, 'Religious love put[s] out religion's eye' (250). But the difference is more ideological than emotional: in both sets of poems basic is a response to the beloved involving – as in Plato – reverence, awe, and a sense of the sacred.

Michelangelo's drawings point to a similar fundamental congruity. Often in Shakespeare a subject is given depth and resonance by a background sense of some mythic or large-scale correspondence that is not specifically articulated: with Hamlet, Orestes, or young Oedipus; with Lear, Job, or Oedipus in old age; or (to shift the terms) with Hamlet, *Weltschmerz* and *Unheimlichkeit* independent of his specific situation; with Iago and Othello, cynicism's hatred of idealism; with Antony's Egypt and Octavius's Rome, the Blakean complementarities energy and reason (the terms are Blake's, the opposition is eternal); with Falstaff a vast cluster of positives and negatives of which the specific invocations of 'Vanity' and 'that old white-bearded Satan' give only a partial notion – and only on one side. No shorthand can more than point to these resonances; and the primary evidence for them is not so much in the texts as in the history of reception – the depths the plays have been felt to possess in an immense variety of cultural situations, often (as in translation or adaptation) independent of their precise articulation. In his drawings Michelangelo points to mythic analogies, which appear in submerged ways in the poems (Ganymede, 59; Tityos, 98; Phaëton, 100). In the Sonnets Shakespeare similarly offers no more than passing reference to myth (WH is self-adoring Narcissus [1: echoes of Ovid], 'the tenth Muse' [38], Adonis or Helen [53]; his perfidious beauty is like 'Eve's apple' [93]). But, as with Michelangelo, there is the sense of capaciously representative feelings. This draws on a philosophical hinterland of large meanings in love (Plato), and (with Shakespeare specifically) the perspective of the wisdom of Solomon (59), a view of time encompassing Pythagorean cycles (59) and the Last Judgement (55), and a sense of generalization implicit in the range of his imagery. Michelangelo's overt uses of myth, in his amplification of poems with drawings, point to an archetypal quality felt in the Shakespeare sequence as a whole. In both sets of poems the manner of exchanges so private that they are as if overheard is combined with a sense of representative experience.

Religion, myth – and gender. Both Michelangelo and Shakespeare worked in contexts regarded by contemporaries as breeding-grounds of 'sodomy' – meaning illicit sexuality of all kinds. In a society in which homosexuality is not regarded as sinful and is not illegal, and men who identify themselves as gay can meet each other openly, the emotional uncertainties that arise between men engaged in relationships of affection brought about by interactions different from those based on settled sexual identities have perhaps become more difficult to conceive. But it may be that the gain in openness of modern sexual *mores* is paid for (contingently, not necessarily) by a loss of fluidity – a fluidity that forces creative grappling with feelings that cannot be absorbed into recognized forms. Both Michelangelo's and Shakespeare's poems show struggles with feelings which, partly because they could not take recognized forms or be understood within recognized expectations, were driven to deep questionings about love. 'Non so se s'è la desïate luce' (76: I do not know if it is the longed-for light); 'What is your substance, whereof are you made?' (Sonnet 53). Whatever their ideal forms might have been, it is a distortion to think of these intense and passionate 'friendships' (there is no fully appropriate word) as (semi-)repressed versions of modern gay relationships: they arose in different ways, and existed in different contexts. With their (variously) religious sense of love, and their broad (mythic, archetypal) resonance, the poems of Michelangelo and Shakespeare also share a portrayal of love between men that is sexual in ways distinctly different from dominant modern assumptions.

Thomas Mann and *Death in Venice*

'Eternal love for boys', Thomas Mann noted in his diary (3 June 1953). He was seventy-seven. Love between men, and particularly the Shakespeare Sonnet situation – love of an older man for a younger – was central to Mann's life and to his work. 'Eternal': he saw this love as a permanent aspect of human experience; and it had played a fundamental part in his own life, beginning when, at fourteen (in 1889), he fell in love with a school-friend, Armin Martens. As often, Mann later wrote the experience into fiction. Martens, Mann's 'first love' ('one more tender, more blissfully painful was never granted me': letter, 19 March 1955), became Hans Hansen, the youth with whom the hero is briefly in love in *Tonio Kröger*. In life Armin Martens was quickly succeeded by Williram (Willri) Timpe, again a contemporary, who was also turned into fiction, as Pribislav Hippe with whom Hans Castorp is briefly fascinated in *The Magic Mountain*. The serious love of Mann's life before his marriage in 1905 was likewise a contemporary, Paul Ehrenberger, with whom Mann was emotionally engaged from 1899 to 1903, and who may (as no other of the men with whom he was infatuated or in love did) have actually become Mann's lover. Much later he referred to his love for Paul as 'that central experience of my heart' (Diary, 6 May 1934). This relationship too was transformed into fiction: Paul is the original of the violinist Rudi Schwerdtfeger, the would-be lover of the composer Adrian Leverkühn, the Faust of *Doctor Faustus*.

With Armin Martens, Willri Timpe, and Paul Ehrenberger Mann was in relationships with contemporaries. While he saw continuities, he also saw important differences between these relationships – feelings prompted in a teenager by a teenager, in a young man by a young man – and feelings prompted in an adult by an adolescent. Here Mann saw the interaction between what is bestowed by the adult's imagination and what is elicited from the youth's real being as unusually complex. More even than is common in erotic relationships, the object of love is constructed by the subject's imagination – constructed as some freer, pre-inhibition version of the adult through whom aspects of a lost self might be recovered; or constructed as less settled in sexual feelings, liminal and in transition – a creatively open child-adult boy-girl, the Shakespearean 'sweet boy', 'master-mistress'. Mann appears also to have seen such relationships as, for him, reawakening the primal experience of erotic attraction, with the penumbra of desires and aspirations that carried with it; the experience from which he had learned love of beauty in art, and an aspiration to give life an intensity compatible with that thirst for beauty. But Mann both sought and resisted explanations, aware that no explanation accounts for the power of the supra-rational, and that there can be many different bases for the experience of every kind of homosexual feeling – bases among which he provocatively included intensified maleness inherent in the militarism of German culture and normal male sexuality when not inhibited by social *mores*.

Whatever their source, after Mann's marriage his homoerotic feelings were directed not towards contemporaries but towards younger men, adolescents, and boys. Of these one of the most important (Mann noted in his diary continuity with 'Paul, Willri and Armin' [11 July 1950]) was a young waiter in a Zurich hotel, Franz Westermayer. After one meeting with 'Franzl' Mann quoted a great exemplar of the 'eternal love for boys' whom he was then reading: 'Nel vostro fiato son le mie parole' (with your breath are my words formed: Michelangelo, Rime 89, to Tommaso); and 'la forza d'un bel viso [a che mi sprona?]' (To what am I spurred by the power of a beautiful face: Rime 279). Franzl epitomized boy-beauty as Muse – and more than Muse: 'insane and passionately maintained enthusiasm for the attraction of male youth, unsurpassed by anything in the world, which lies at the basis of everything' (Diary, 6 August 1950). But after Paul Ehrenberger, the relationship with a young man to which Mann gave greatest importance was with Klaus Heuser, whom he knew for a short period in 1927. Mann was fifty-two, Klaus Heuser seventeen. Mann's diary for 1927 is lost, and his reflections on the relationship are known only from later entries – in 1942

(20 February): 'beloved lips that I kissed – it was there, I had it too, I'll be able to tell myself when I die'; and in 1934 (6 May) he described his feelings for Klaus Heuser as 'probably humanly proper [menschlich regelrecht], and because of this normality I feel my life more strongly integrated into the canonical [ins Kanonische eingeordnet] than through marriage and children'. By such experiences his life was brought to accord with a recognized pattern – a striking conclusion, but Mann probably had in mind what he elsewhere described as an 'emotional tendency that is as old as the human race' (public letter of 1930 arguing for the decriminalization in Germany of homosexual acts in private between consenting adults). Relationships differently emotional and sexual with a woman and with a young man (a sequence of young men): the pattern of the Shakespeare Sonnets is the pattern which, when life is not pressed into other shapes by constricting social norms, Mann thought 'Kanonische eingeordnet'.

Mann attributed to his feelings for Klaus Heuser the argument about loyalty in love added as a prefatory paragraph to his essay on Kleist's *Amphitryon*.

> We meet a face we love, and after some looking at it during which our feeling is confirmed, we are parted from it. Forgetting is certain . . . What we have left is only the certainty that each new meeting of our nature with this living manifestation will certainly renew our feeling, make us love it again, or, more properly, love it still. (*Essays of Three Decades*, 202)

'This living manifestation': while we may forget each loved individual, we encounter through successive incarnations the revelation of a power that cannot be simply identified but which prompts the same reaction – brings into being that responsiveness in our nature which is one form of what we call love. Mann's paradoxical argument is that, though it may involve apparent disloyalty when different people prompt in us the same response, fundamentally love is loyal – not to an individual, but to an idea. All the boys in whom the god resides are avatars of one archetypal boy. WH is Southampton-Pembroke-WillieHughes – and Adonis.

In no boy was the god present more resonantly for Mann than in Baron Wladyslaw Moes, whom he saw while holidaying in Venice for a week in 1911. His fascination with this young Polish aristocrat was the germ of *Death in Venice*. Born in late 1900, Wladyslaw Moes was ten when Mann encountered him, though he may have appeared older (Mann's wife, Katia, remembered him as 'about thirteen'): in fiction 'Tadzio' (Mann never knew his actual name) became 'about fourteen'. The central character of the novella, Gustav von Aschenbach, who becomes obsessed with the boy, is semi-autobiographical. Like Mann he is a writer, his father patrician and disciplined, his mother Bohemian and artistic. Aschenbach's works are planned or uncompleted projects of Mann's; the examples of the hero type Aschenbach favours correspond to figures in Mann's completed works; the critical judgement reported from a 'shrewd commentator' on Aschenbach (261) is from an early critique of Mann. But Aschenbach is over fifty; Mann was thirty-five. Aschenbach is a future self into which the author needs not to degenerate. The way beyond Aschenbach's situation – respectability bounded by convention, simplistic moralism, writing neutralized to textbook model – is the embrace of prohibited beauty. Aschenbach does not choose his forbidden passion. A desire for emotionally disruptive adventure is prompted by an uncanny encounter; ultimately he is taken over by passions too powerful for the exercise of his will. The novella mimes through Aschenbach the process of self-discovery that writing was for Mann, exploring the relation of emotion, release, and poetry to intellect, control, and prose – the contest expressed in myth between what to Mann were the Nietzschean as well as classical antagonists, Dionysus and Apollo.

'What is your substance, whereof are you made, / That millions of strange shadows on you tend?' (Sonnet 53). *Death in Venice* offers an exploration of the meanings of spiritual-erotic response and a fully imagined experience of spiritual-erotic obsession. The mystery of the boy's emotional power for Aschenbach is central. Mann interrogates it in a spectrum of ways: he relates it to the beauty of Greek art, and to boy-love in Greek mythology; he relates it to the understanding of human beauty in Platonic philosophy, in which erotic response is a distraction from the ultimate by the immediate, a mistaking of 'shadow' for 'substance'; and he relates it to the converse, a highly physical eroticism understood as a sacred power. 'Or do you think rather (I leave it to you to decide) . . .' (340): so Mann's Socrates to his boy, Phaedrus; and so Mann to the reader. All the ways of understanding the effect of the boy that Mann presents have some validity for Aschenbach – and some analogy with the qualities that fascinate and compel Shakespeare in WH.

Most simply Tadzio is associated with Greek sculpture generally, and specifically with the Spinario (boy pulling a thorn), epitome in classical art of the innocently eroticized boy-girl. Like WH (Adonis), he resembles beautiful youths loved by the gods – Zeus's Ganymede, Apollo's Hyacinthus. Like WH, beauty makes him self-absorbed – Narcissus, lost in wonder at his own image. Like WH (Beauty, Truth [14, 54, 101]), he has the effect of some ultimate power: Tadzio resembles Eros himself. As a result of the sense of sacred presence he creates, Aschenbach experiences Greek myth as living religion – the sun as Apollo, sea as Oceanus, nature as Pan-esque, dawn as Eos. Tadzio emerging from the sea is as 'a tale of the origins of form and of the birth of the gods' (290). These are Aschenbach's perceptions, but there is not always a distance between Aschenbach and his narrator. Even when Mann ironizes Aschenbach's response he never does so entirely: it is at once both 'ludicrous and sacred' (313: lächerlich und heilig).

In philosophy Tadzio specifically recalls the discussions of Love in *Symposium* and *Phaedrus*, and more generally Plato's theory of Forms. Though Aschenbach twists Plato to his own purposes, Mann is not only characterizing his central figure. Plato probes what Mann sees as legitimate ways of understanding beauty and love. Through Plato Mann asks whether Aschenbach's adventure of the emotions is ultimately physical or spiritual – and finds that it is both. Mann is true to his Greek sources in extracting from the discourses of Socrates an erotic subtext that their primary arguments negate.

In Platonic discourse Tadzio is 'a model and mirror' (304: Stand-bild und Spiegel). But whereas in Plato the beauty of the beloved offers a recollection or intimation of that perfection to which the material world provides pointers, but not more, to Aschenbach's ecstatic state Tadzio is the thing itself, 'Form as a thought of God' (304: die Form als Gottesgedanken). Aschenbach's reverie mixes fragmentary recreations of the *Phaedrus* with Plutarch's Platonist *Erotikos* (*Dialogue on Love*: testing the contention that 'there is only one genuine love, the love of boys' [§750]). Modified recreation gives his thought an intoxicated turn that is, in Platonic terms, delusory. Half-recognizing his error, Aschenbach indulges the delicious narcotic-stimulant of the love god: like WH, Tadzio is 'Beauty itself' (304). But this is not simply delusion. The narrator is not a quiescent student in the Platonic Academy, nor need the reader aspire to be one. Aschenbach recreates the discussion between Socrates and Phaedrus because he is reliving the experiences that underlie Platonic doctrine. Grappling with thoughts based on real experiences, he is a model for readers: he comes up with real meanings, which are his own – meanings drawn from his reading, integrated with his experiences.

Socrates is presented as what the sceptical reader of Plato may find him – not dispassionate but highly engaged, a 'sly wooer' (305, verschlagene Hofmacher) whose ideas are 'alive with all the mischie-vousness and most secret voluptuousness of the heart' (306). His thought is a way of drawing to him the beloved young man, Agathon or Phaedrus. Like Aschenbach's thought, Socrates' philosophy is an activity shaped by erotic pressures. And as with thinking, so with writing: 'thou art all my art' (Sonnet 78). Under the immediate impact of Tadzio's beauty Aschenbach 'had never known so clearly that Eros dwells in language' (306). The emblem of his aspiration as a writer is Michelangelesque: his visionary prose is to be the Zeus-eagle that exalts Ganymede-Tadzio. He is really enabled by his experience: 'The writer's joy is the thought that can become emotion, the emotion that can wholly become a thought' (306). This is the narrator's view, as it is Mann's, and it is what Aschenbach achieves. On the terms on which Aschenbach receives it, the experience of Tadzio's beauty releases in him as a human being forces that rejuvenate him as a writer.

'The thought that can become emotion, the emotion that can become thought': the idea is derived from an epigram ('Rückblick') by August von Platen. Platen is one of several semi-submerged homosexual presences in Mann's novella, and the most important. Aschenbach is reminded of Platen's Venetian Sonnets as he approaches Venice – an implication that homosexual feeling is more an aspect of his sensibility than he recognizes. Platen's Sonnets include a poem on Shakespeare's Sonnets, admiring how struggles with love for the young man transform suffering into beauty; and Platen is a significant figure in the afterlife of Shakespeare's Sonnets, one of the first homosexual writers to take up the sequence for the cultural validation it could give to an illicit sexuality. In Mann's essay on Platen (1930, *Essays of Three Decades*), he argues that in his poetry Platen chose traditional forms that dealt with sexual love for young men (the Pindaric ode, the Persian ghazal, the Renaissance sonnet) because this gave the feelings a sense of being traditional and time-honoured, permanent aspects of men's experience of love and desire. He argues too that homosexuality was fundamental to Platen's writing, proposing that 'the degree and kind of a man's sexuality permeates the very loftiest heights of his intellect' (*Essays of Three Decades*, 265: the idea – evidently applicable to Mann's own work – is from Nietzsche [*Beyond Good and Evil*, aphorism 75]). That Platen could not act on his feelings regularly betrayed him, Mann supposes, to young men whose qualities were at best partial versions of what Platen ('a Don Quixote of love') believed he found in them. But this is not simple delusion in love. Marking the connection between Platen and *Death in Venice* – and arguably with Shakespeare's Sonnets – Mann makes in his own person the observation left in the novella to Socrates: 'the god is in the loving, not the beloved' (*Essays of Three Decades*, 266; *Death in Venice*, 306).

Socrates re-enters *Death in Venice* for Aschenbach's final Platonic reverie, which is again made up from *Symposium* and *Phaedrus*. Delirious from cholera, degraded by infatuation, Aschenbach is half-asleep: his discourse has the logic of a dream. Nevertheless, though his thoughts are again freely recreated from their sources, he gives an accurate representation of Socrates on the dangers to Wisdom of Beauty, extrapolating dangers for artists particularly, who 'cannot tread the path of Beauty without Eros . . . appointing himself as [their] guide' (340). So Aschenbach has found. Eros is his guide, and Eros destroys him. But the god first gives him back the ability to integrate in writing emotion and thought. And though Aschenbach is destroyed, it is not by Eros alone. He is destroyed by the interaction of Eros with the shell of himself he had half become. Mann's fiction is a moral fable, but it is not applicable to art, artists, and readers unconditionally.

If Eros is a dangerous god, even more dangerous is Dionysus. Through Dionysus Mann acknowledges what Aschenbach suppresses – sexual desire. His feeling for Tadzio is not only about beauty, art, and the transcendental, and it cannot be entirely understood in the terms offered by Socrates. In a dream of violently orgiastic sexuality Aschenbach worships Dionysus. He recognizes an alliance between his passion and the criminal concealment of cholera in Venice: passion and crime thrive alike on disorder. The dream is the nadir of his degradation. But it is not simply negative. Aschenbach's early novel castigating sympathy with the abyss characterized his limitations. The reader need not repeat Aschenbach's error. Mann acknowledges through the dream that the Socratic view of boy-love responds to only part of Aschenbach's experience. Mann thought of art as having a kinship with the forbidden, the metaphysically and emotionally 'criminal'. Aschenbach's emotional adventure in all its aspects is necessary to his creativity.

The full presence in Aschenbach of what happens to him is in its way heroic. Much later in his life, commenting on a situation that he must have conceived as analogous to that of the novella, Mann probed with Michelangelo the effect of unremitting erotic sublimation.

> What is the source of the constant melancholia of a creator blessed by heaven with overwhelming powers of invention? I think that what provides the explanation is an immense and oppressive sensuousness, constantly struggling towards the pure, the spiritual, the divine, understanding itself always as a transcendental longing. ('Die Erotik Michelangelo's', 1950)

'Understanding itself', and misunderstanding itself: the longings were not only transcendental – as Michelangelo occasionally admitted. Plato recognized in Beauty forms of knowledge beyond what can be thought of as sublimated desire, and Mann accepted that. A post-Freudian translation of all passionate aspiration into sex is not for him. But nor is Michelangelo's continual translation of desire into religious feeling. *Death in Venice* – in this more congruent with Shakespeare than with Michelangelo – acknowledges the gam-ut, from Plato to Dionysus.

Not fully congruent with either Shakespeare or Michelangelo, however, is the novella's particular mode of older-younger man relationship. *Death in Venice* does not present a relationship in the manner of those of the Sonnets and the Rime developed over a period of years, incorporating a wide range of intimate experience. It is a distinctive condition of Aschenbach's feelings for Tadzio that 'desire is born of defective knowledge' (311: die Sehnsucht ist ein Erzeugnis mangelhafter Erkenntnis). His exchanges with the boy confined to the visual, Aschenbach interprets by intuition, and so is free to indulge projections onto Tadzio without (as he recognizes) the sobering correctives that more complete knowledge might bring. How far this distinctive condition defines the relationship is questionable. If in love knowledge is never other than incomplete, defective knowledge is a ubiquitous ground for the birth and rebirth of desire. While Shakespeare's Sonnets at times register a sense of identification so powerful that the beloved is conceived as a second self, WH is also almost permanently Other. Love in the Sonnets may be temporarily plenitude and stasis. More often it is falling back into the dynamic defective state from which desire is reborn.

And as with Shakespeare and his aristocratic youth, as with Michelangelo and the young patrician Tommaso, the distance in age that separates Aschenbach and Tadzio is compounded by a difference of class. Tadzio's historical original (though Mann did not know this) was an aristocrat ('baron'). Tadzio's class is not so definitely marked, but the gendered treatment of the boy and his sisters, the formalized behaviour supervised by their French governess, Tadzio's costume and manners, the mother's extraordinary pearls and her elegance suggesting 'aristocratic values' (282: Bestandteil der Vornehmenheit) – all this implies the status to which Aschenbach (with his pride in a late-bestowed 'von') does not belong by birth, but to which he aspires. Class emphasizes the barriers between the man and the boy, but it also plays a part in what attracts Aschenbach to Tadzio (his aloofness and self-possession, his disdain for the commonplace). That this pattern of barrier-and-allure is common to Mann, Michelangelo, and Shakespeare suggests that aristocracy is experienced as symbolizing both the exaltation of the object of desire and the difficulty of its attainment.

Among contemporaries, the writers of whose work Mann was most aware as exploring the nature and meanings of boy-love were Stefan George and André Gide. George translated into German the complete sequence of Shakespeare's Sonnets (1909), with a preface about their 'übergeschletlichen Liebe' – 'sex-transcending love'. The idea is open to interpretation, but on no view is sex-transcending sex-bypassing. Describing it as equally foolish to criticize or to defend 'what one of the greatest of mortals thought good', George does not discuss; but 'übergeschletlichen Liebe' apparently meant love directed to the whole person, body and soul, independent of any biochemistry of sexual drive, and free to direct and fulfil itself in ways that recognized that independence. It is a defence of boy-love that, for obvious legal reasons, is expressed obliquely. When George completed his Sonnets translation he had recently written his own sequence of love poems to a youth, Maximilian Kronberger. George met Maximilian in 1902 when he was fourteen. The boy died (of meningitis) in 1904. The aim of George's *Maximin: Ein Gedenkbuch* (1907) is to give expression to the divine properties incarnated in Maximilian. The circle of which George was the central figure was consciously Platonist. As with Michelangelo, the physical expression of desire is presented by George as a misunderstanding of love's passionate aspiration towards the transcendent. The congruence with one side of *Death in Venice* is clear. George's translation makes evident the connection of the mode of feeling, as he saw it, with Shakespeare.

Gide is George's antithesis, entirely willing to see and celebrate desire in relation to boys as erotic. Mann was (later) impressed by the boldness and honesty of Gide's frank treatment of the subject in his autobiography, *Si le grain ne meurt* (1924), but he did not endorse Gide's erotic attitude. 'Annoyed at him because of his much too direct sexually aggressive behaviour toward youth, without respect, deference toward it, without being ashamed of his age.' His objection was not (as with Michelangelo) that Gide misunderstood his feelings (that they were really for the Form of Beauty, or the god of which the boy was an avatar), but that to act on them as Gide did was 'actually loveless' (Diary, 6 October 1951). It is congruent with this that Mann apparently accepted George's criticism that 'in *Death in Venice* the highest is drawn down into the realm of decadence' (letter, 4 July 1920) – that the divine properties of Tadzio might have been presented more exclusively in terms of myth and symbol; and that Aschenbach's response, insofar as it is presented naturalistically, appears too straightforwardly erotic. It is the *Death in Venice* combination of these elements in the Shakespeare Sonnets that post-Freudian reading is most prone to understand too simply – relatively at ease with what to Gide was revolutionary; all but deaf to Michelangelo's and George's Platonism.

Mann wrote about his novella to a distant acquaintance, Carl Weber (letter, 4 July 1920). Weber was involved in an educational movement that drew on the model of ancient Greece, conscious that 'gymnos' meant 'naked' and that the teachings of the gymnasium included appreciation in a philosophical context of the beauty of the male body. Describing his aim in *Death in Venice* as 'an equilibrium of sensuality and morality', Mann acknowledges that the initial impulse was 'hymnic', but that the 'intoxicate song turned into a moral fable'. This development is present, he concedes, in a problematic relation in the novella between symbolism and realism: affirmation of Eros in the myth; undermining of Eros by the central character – and by the author. In a discussion of homosexuality more generally Mann adds, 'I see nothing unnatural and a good deal of instructive significance, a good deal of higher humanity, in the tenderness of mature masculinity for lovelier and frailer masculinity'. He cites Hölderlin's 'Sokrates und Alcibiades' – 'one of the world's most beautiful love poems': 'Wer das Tiefste gedacht, liebt das Lebendigste' (he who the deepest has thought loves what is most alive). 'This wonderful poem', Mann comments, 'contains the whole justification of the emotional tendency in question, and the whole explanation of it, which is mine also'. It is the conclusion of an argument in which he presents the novella's form of homosexual feeling as congruent with and a key to understanding more general desires and aspirations. The whole relationship of life and mind is 'erotic without clarification of the sexual polarity' – that is, erotic, but not on the model of heterosexual Eros: it is 'an eternal tension without resolution'. Aschenbach's obsession properly understood (by the novella, not entirely by the character) is with a revelation. Tadzio, like WH, is its Muse – a provocation to comprehensive feeling-thought and the stimulus to giving that feeling-thought form.

Benjamin Britten, *Death in Venice*

Britten's opera, *Death in Venice* (1973), follows Mann's novella closely and replicates much of it directly, taking over most of its narrative, characters, and themes. Britten retains Aschenbach's struggle between

Platonic and erotic visions of his experience, and, as in Mann, Tadzio is set in a context of Greek culture. There are also changes. These arise partly from the change of medium, partly from emphases given by Britten. Music-theatre makes a more direct appeal to the emotions and the senses than prose fiction: the audience is drawn into Aschenbach's emotional states. Music also characterizes the context of Aschenbach's emotional adventure – Venice as ambiguous (cross-rhythms for water/instability; brass and bells for stone/conviction); Venice as visionary (a mysterious chord sequence ['Serenissima', score §25]; an expansive melody associated with the sea [§59]); Venice as corruptly commercial (melodic and rhythmic cliché for a barber's chatter; distortions of trite popular song for strolling players).

Theatre gives unmediated access to Aschenbach, in whom Britten combines features of Mann's character and narrator. Unmediated access means that the audience, when not simply drawn in by music's emotional power, is guided through channels more open to interpretation than narrative commentary – dramatic contextualization; text-music interaction. Theatre also means an unmediated view of Tadzio, whom Britten – reflecting the boy's non-speaking role in the novella – made a dancer. One of the aims in using dance was 'to externalise Aschenbach's habit of poeticising the events in which he could not partake' (Myfanwy Piper, the opera's librettist, in Herbert, *The Operas of Benjamin Britten*). Dance also has the effect of poeticizing those events for the audience, and so justifying Aschenbach's view of them. The audience participates in Aschenbach's admiration of beauty – beauty not (as in Mann) of sickly delicacy, but of the trained body, as in the Greek gymnasium, the beauty of the young male body in dance. For Mann, despite a sense of the presence of 'Eros in the word', prose can only describe the effects of physical beauty. Dance exhibits it. And in its energy and physicality dance engages directly with the erotic. Choreography that responds to the possibilities offered by Britten's score will combine – as many modern choreographers have – the disciplines of classical ballet with the freedoms of Isadora Duncan and Martha Graham. Dance both supports Aschenbach's

Socratic sense-making (classical disciplines: Tadzio, like WH, is impersonal Beauty) and embodies the promptings to his more sexual
response (modern freedoms: Tadzio, like WH, is an object of desire).
Tadzio as dancer combines the novella's polarities, which are only more
evident in the opera: Apollonian discipline and Dionysiac release.

Unmediated access to character; the emotional power of music
and dance; music-text interaction: much of this follows from the
change of medium. All of it Britten manipulates in his own ways, in
effect to reactivate Mann's originating 'hymnic' impulse, making his
Death in Venice, far from a moral fable, a paean of praise in song and
dance to the frenzy of love inspired by beauty.

Britten also made choices not consequent on the change of
medium. One role is added, a role derived from Mann implicitly, the
Voice of Apollo. It makes Mann's Nietzschean conflict in Aschenbach
more explicit. Figures in Mann managing the progress of Aschen-
bach-Everyman on his journey towards Death are connected more
emphatically by combining them in multiple roles for one singer: the
graveyard-encountered Traveller, the Gondolier-Charon with his
gondola-coffin, the Leader of the Strolling Players, herald of the
cholera. Britten also draws together in this role characters Mann does
not link: the Elderly Fop, the Hotel Barber, the Voice of Dionysus,
and the Hotel Manager – another figure of Death, disposing of all
entrances and exits. And Britten brings out (from Mann, but more
obviously) the connection of these figures with Hermes, guider of
souls in the Underworld. The uncanny and sinister but also mocking
and ironic figures moving Aschenbach towards death are brought
together in a unity that reinforces the dark underside of his experience. As in the Sonnets, the radiance of beauty, 'like a jewel hung in
ghastly night' (27), is intensified by the darkness that threatens to
engulf its momentary perfection.

As with Mann, Aschenbach was for Britten an autobiographical
figure. Even more than Mann, Britten's emotional life featured
a succession of teenage boys – Wulff Scherchen, eighteen when he
was the inspiration for Britten's *Young Apollo* (1938); David

Hemmings, thirteen when Britten wrote for him the part of Miles in
The Turn of the Screw (1954); and many other boys whose holidays
with Britten included sharing his bed, joint bathing in a specially
contrived double shower, naked swimming, and other pleasures,
which they all remembered later as innocent delights in which Britten participated boyishly himself. Britten's correspondence shows
that with several of these boys he played the role of *erastes* to *eromenos*
in the chaste Socratic manner, and with some of them, like Aschenbach, he could say (and did say, more or less explicitly), 'I love you'.
Scarcely needed in the Greek gymnasium, Britten's contrivances for
physical freedom and intimacy were perhaps (mutatis mutandis)
those of homosexuals in any age of prohibition, though, in order to
ensure a continuous flow of inspiration from Tadzio-figures, Britten
may have gone further than most in organizing them. On the theory
of Oscar Wilde that WH was a boy actor, the Shakespearean theatre
would have provided inspiration for the Sonnets in an abundance
that rendered contrivance unnecessary.

Britten described *Death in Venice* as representing 'everything . . .
I have stood for' (Mitchell, *Death in Venice*, 207). Everything he had
stood for? Boy-love in a Platonist context; the validity of homosexual
love in a general way (limited decriminalization in England came
about only shortly before Britten began the opera); and love of and
dedication to beauty as seen in Tadzio and in the cultural contexts
established by the opera – music, dance, literature, philosophy, with
Venice also suggesting painting, architecture, and the arts more generally in association with religion. It was the last of many works implying the validity of homosexual feeling in reworkings of iconic cultural
figures, including *Seven Sonnets of Michelangelo* (1940, all but one
poems addressed to Tommaso), 'Sokrates und Alcibiades', so admired
by Mann (*Sechs Hölderlin Fragmente*, 1958), and Shakespeare's Sonnet
of insomniac obsession, 'When most I wink' (*Nocturne*, 1958).

As in Mann, Aschenbach's problem as a writer is that he conceives
the aesthetic too narrowly, purely in terms of form and beauty.
Having renounced sympathy with the outcast he does not let in

enough life. The situation was and was not Britten's. While Britten could think of his work in Aschenbach's aesthetic terms, this was not at the expense of ideological engagements. In his work sympathy for the outsider is central: he writes as a homosexual and a pacifist. Aschenbach's art, with its etiolated formalist aesthetic and negative attitude to passion, has renounced sympathy with the human condition. *Death in Venice* shows Aschenbach re-humanizing to become the kind of figure his art has eschewed.

Tadzio provides the experience of visionary passion that forces life back into Aschenbach's art and releases his blocked creativity. The boy's extraordinary aura is endorsed by his music – a distinctive spread chord scored with exotic beauty for quasi-oriental tuned percussion. As in Mann, Aschenbach both struggles to make sense of his feelings and resists understanding them: they are intellectual-aesthetic (Tadzio is 'the soul of Greece'); they are paternal (Aschenbach feels 'a father's pleasure'). But despite Aschenbach's evasions, his feelings are presented positively because they release his creativity. Britten adds an emphatic ratification: a sporting contest, over which Apollo presides and which Tadzio wins, exhibits physical beauty as 'the only form / Of spirit that our eyes can see'; beauty brings 'Reflections of Divinity . . . to the outcast soul' (§158–59) – outcast (on a Platonist view) simply by virtue of being in this world. Britten emphasizes the exaltation of the vision. The audience is drawn into Aschenbach's ecstatic response.

But it is as result of this that Aschenbach is not able to 'normalise' – that is, de-sexualize – his relationship with Tadzio. He cannot 'become friends' with Transcendent Beauty. 'So longing passes back and forth between life and the mind' (§186): Aschenbach's conclusion is not from the novella but from Mann's commentary (his letter to Carl Weber). As Britten knew, it gives Mann's reason for understanding homosexual love as analogous to a general dynamic between experience and feeling-thought. Britten incorporates this reflection – for Aschenbach as Everyman – before plunging Aschenbach into his struggles with the relation of the visionary to the erotic. Aschenbach's feeling for Tadzio is a response to the substance of which the beautiful boy is a shadow – but it is not that only. It is also a response to the vehicle: 'I love you' (§188).

Despite Britten's ultimate intention of qualifying some of Mann's negativities, he does not shirk them. As in Mann, Aschenbach discovers Venice's criminal secret and relishes its congruity with his prohibited passion. As in Mann, he takes on the identity of the Elderly Fop: temporarily vision is overwhelmed by sex. But other elements suggest different meanings. Britten finally implies more definitely than Mann that the Platonic solution – that the individual beauty through which the divine was first glimpsed must be left behind – denies a valid part of the whole: it denies a form of love that integrates, as the artist will always wish to, intellect and feeling.

'Longing passes back and forth between life and the mind': Britten's lyrical setting of this crucial idea lays the basis for a musical commentary on the action. The theme becomes the upper line of a double ground bass running throughout Aschenbach's pursuit of Tadzio (§211–32). The lower line of this ground bass is a variant of 'I love you' – 'sacred . . . not dishonourable, even in these circumstances' (§193). Aschenbach's obsession, the music tells us, is driven by large forces: Tadzio is both a particular boy and an all-encompassing Eros. The music in effect endorses Aschenbach's claim that his possessed state is congruent with the heroic stance required of the artist (§234).

The dream of Dionysus is ambivalent. As god of the games Apollo was encouragingly Socratic: 'Love that beauty causes / Is frenzy god-inspired, / Nearer to the gods / Than sanity' (§157). Socrates discusses love in just these terms, as divine madness, in *Phaedrus*. Apollo endorses the visionary, creative response into which Aschenbach is released by the games, which affirmed (from Mann) the artist's central ability, to unite feeling and thought (§178, 183). But in the dream the unloosened bridle of Apollo encourages a return to the ideas that caused the creative blockage from which Aschenbach, by his response to Tadzio, escaped: 'Reject the abyss; . . . love beauty, form'. Unbridled Dionysus, however, is no answer. Aschenbach may not be able to resist Tadzio sexualized ('Do what you will with me'), but the climax of the dance of Dionysiac revellers is Tadzio's chord stripped of its numinous aura. It conveys the horror of Tadzio's desecration into an object of purely sexual desire. Still, in this battle for the soul of Aschenbach the urgings of Dionysus ('He who denies the god denies his nature') are more persuasive than the discredited offerings of Apollo. And the musical recall of the opening scene (§20, 280) implies that Aschenbach's dream is a destiny: this is the adventure he unconsciously recognized that his soul needed.

The final unresolved questionings from a Platonic position (§308–10) echo the injunctions of Apollo about beauty and detach-ment, the terms of what Aschenbach began by trying to escape. The Dionysiac dream of passion may not offer an answer, but the reasonings of philosophy too circle round without a resolution. The music's comment is a fugue on the expansive 'sea' melody, and a return of the double ground bass: Venice has been a place of vision. Aschenbach experienced both love for a particular boy and intuitions of an all-encompassing Eros (§311, 317). Aschenbach dies, but the music of the closing tableau does not imply defeat. The Tadzio motif is combined with the theme of Aschenbach's released creativity, his ecstatic realization prompted by the games (§325). The unresolved dissonance over which the two themes are played is the aural equiva-lent of an open question.

Britten's opera is not simply Mann's novella in another form. There is more light (the Games) and more darkness (the multiple figures of Death). Aschenbach is more sympathetic, his obsession more positive, his death more clearly not a defeat. Britten implies a Nietzschean critique of the Socratic sublimation that Mann pre-sented with less of a decisive steer. In life Britten had addressed the dilemmas of his sexuality differently from Mann. Like Mann, he lived in a long-term relationship, one even more central to his creative life, with the singer, Peter Pears. But more than Mann, who kept his relations with young men and boys largely at a distance,

Britten engaged in emotional relationships with a succession of ado-lescents, some of whom he treated as Muses. As with Mann, all the boys are one archetypal Boy. Of them all (with Pears) Britten could say, as Shakespeare says of WH, 'thou art all my art'.

With opera-ballet myth is not – as Stefan George objected of Mann's novella – drawn down to the implications of realism. Tadzio is more a symbol than a character. No more than the novella does the opera deal with the Sonnets' struggle to engage with a beloved whom the lover experiences as another self but has also to recognize as recalcitrantly not-self. But as a sympathetic account of spiritual-erotic obsession the opera is a study of one effect of that recognition: as in the Sonnets, the lover is possessed, insomniac, a 'slave' (57, 58: 'do with me what you will'). Then, like the Sonnets, and more emphatically than the novella, through the various incarnations of the graveyard-Traveller who attends Aschenbach, and the concealed plague analogous to his illicit passion, the opera associates love and death. WH's beauty teaches meditation on time and transience; Aschenbach's response to Tadzio is intensified by the multiple shadows of 'sad mortality' (65) that attend him. And just as the hors-ily carnal 'neigh' of desire (51) is celebrated as an aspect of the 'religious love' 'consecrate' to WH, so the experience of Aschenbach is at once erotic and spiritual: his struggle is to integrate the two. At least as it is usually understood, Platonism is not enough. Britten conveys the presence of the erotic within the spiritual by means at once sensuous and intellectual – beauty of sound and of structure in music, beauty of body and of plastic geometry in dance. And, like Shakespeare, Britten also gives full weight to the possible desecration (de-sacralization) of beauty by desire: 'the expense of spirit in a waste of shame'. Shakespeare's good and evil angels (144), his loves of com-fort and despair, WH and the Dark Lady, are both present in Aschen-bach's responses to Tadzio. But the main analogy with the Sonnets lies in Britten's restoring the novella's originating 'hymnic' impulse. Eros may be in the word, but it is not so readily in the words of prose, however beautifully written. Like the Sonnets, the opera embodies an irregular recognition of beauty as well as celebrating a prohibited love.

Death in Venice is about boy-love. That is its subject. But, as in the Sonnets, the subject is treated with a depth and fullness that opens out beyond its narrative surface. Britten presents a particular form of homosexual experience in terms that imply its applicability to sexual love and love of beauty more generally. In Britten's *Peter Grimes*, Grimes, repudiated by his community, is a surrogate for all persecuted outsiders. Aschenbach's struggles are more specifically projected, but his efforts to understand passions the irregularity of which forces self-examination can be surrogate for anyone whose experience of love does not fall in with the accepted terms of romantic or erotic expectation. In this the boy-love opera is fundamentally congruent with the Sonnets to WH and to the Dark Lady.

Derek Jarman, *The Angelic Conversation*

The reader will always have his or her part to do, just as much as I have had mine. I seek less to state or display any theme or thought, and more to bring you, reader, into the atmosphere of the theme or thought – there to pursue your own flight. (Walt Whitman, *A Backward Glance o'er Travel'd Roads*)

Derek Jarman's *The Angelic Conversation* (1985) is, in intention, a queer film about the Sonnets – 'queer', not 'gay'. 'Gay' Jarman rejected. Gay is either/or, simplifying and optimistic: there are homosexuals and there are heterosexuals, and being homosexual is okay. Whereas (in Jarman's view) everybody is (or could be) queer – that is, all human sexuality is potentially multifarious; 'normal' patterns are a cultural imposition. This is not (as 'gay' implies) okay: for those who do not suppress it, it is both wonderful and painful. Shakespeare, the central icon of English literary culture, did not suppress it. Like Jarman's film of *The Tempest* (1979), *The Angelic Conversation* is loving and respectful towards this reclaimed queer Shakespeare and iconoclastic towards Shakespeare sanitized for culture (heterosexual-bourgeois-decorative), heritage, and education. The film is an intensification of the Sonnets: sexual love between men is presented directly. But in its way the film is also a narrowing – not so diversely 'queer' as the Sonnets themselves. The narrative of the Sonnets disappears, and with it much of their range of sexual experiences: there is no gap of age or class between the male protagonists, no Dark Lady, no rival poet, and little of the jealousy, bitterness, irony, and self-loathing of the poems. However, while there is also nothing from the early group of sonnets urging the young man to defy Time by having children, one issue from that sequence, Narcissism, does complicate the apparent reciprocities of love. And the film is, like the Sonnets, intensely aware of Time – as a threat to beauty and to love, and potentially to everything that gives life value.

Though there is no Dark Lady there is an (unseen) female presence – Judi Dench, who reads the poems. Jarman chose a female reader because he did not want the poems to appear to come from either of the protagonists, so as to maintain an equal balance between them. Judi Dench's slow, expressive readings – not responsive to the full range of possible inflections of the words, often smoothing out undercurrents of bitterness or irony – match perfectly the overall visual treatment, regularly giving full value to the words in a caressing delivery expressing love and desire, which thereby acquire a feminine inflection. And, like WH, the young men are feminized, by the absence of some usual markers of masculinity and the presence of some usual markers of femininity.

The film's title refers to Jarman's interest in the Elizabethan magus, John Dee. Dee was a mathematician, astrologer, and antiquary, who was also actively interested in alchemy, magic (not sharply distinguished from science), and communication with spirits – his 'angelic conversations'. The writings and activities of Dee were known to Jarman through the work of Frances Yates and her associate, Peter French, by whom the serious nature of Dee's work and its connection to networks of Elizabethan semi-secret intellectual life were re-evaluated for a modern audience. Dee is a presence behind both Marlowe's Doctor Faustus and Shakespeare's Prospero. An insider, directly connected to the Elizabethan ruling class and to Queen Elizabeth herself (with whom he appears in Jarman's *Jubilee* [1977]), he was also an outsider with interests and activities that were – like those of Jarman's queer Shakespeare – dangerous.

Jarman began shooting the material which turned into *The Angelic Conversation* with no intention of using Shakespeare's Sonnets. But though the idea of using the poems occurred to him only at a late stage of the shooting, the material was edited with this intention. Though extended sequences are without text, the Sonnets are the most important aspects of the sound track, and for most viewers will govern interpretation of much of the imagery. Whatever the genesis of the use of Shakespeare's poems, in effect, *The Angelic Conversation* is an interpretation of the Sonnets. The film is lyric and non-narrative, but there is a broad structure to the action, which begins with the two main protagonists separate in situations of trial or oppression, and brings them together in expressions of mutual affection. In a coda they again appear separate, but without a return to the earlier landscapes of unhappiness and frustration.

'Derek Jarman takes fourteen of Shakespeare's sonnets as a basis for a visual celebration of the senses – intensely homoerotic, strangely chaste, and vividly illustrative of the deeper, mystical interpretation its title suggests. In the Western mystical tradition, the ardent seeker must come to terms with his passions and master the outer world of the elements. He then fervently invokes this guardian angel (genius, *daimon* or inner self) as a lover calls the beloved, culminating in the *mystical knowledge and conversation of the holy guardian angel* in which the adept is enthroned in the seat of his own soul.' This is the guidance about interpretation offered (anonymously) by the British Film Institute videotape publication of *The Angelic Conversation*. It relates the film to other Jarman work of the 1980s, particularly the immediately following *Caravaggio* (1986). One aspect of the Sonnets this emphasizes is what J. B. Leishman called their 'un-Platonic hyperbole': WH is the focus for aspiration towards beauty, truth, spiritual elevation, the ideal, but this is accomplished, not by the gradual negation of the senses, but through them. Jarman himself gave a more open interpretative lead: the film 'does not dictate to the audience: [it] allows the mind to wander and draw its own conclusions' (Tony Peake, *Derek Jarman*, 334). His attitude to the freedom of the viewer is congruent with his own attitude as a sometimes freewheeling, take-what-you-will reader of the Sonnets – the attitude proposed by Whitman as in accord with the nature of creative reading.

The film has an epigraph from Sonnet 151: 'Love is too young to know what conscience is, / Yet who knows not conscience is born of love' – love in the form of sexual desire ('too young' because Cupid is a boy) is so powerful a force that it overwhelms the sense of right and wrong, but the intense and sensitive reflectiveness that love engenders ultimately develops the moral feelings. How far this is genuinely a key to the film's treatment of love is open to question. One way of reading the film overall is as implying rather that homosexual love is forced to develop through burdens of consciousness that heterosexual love does not have to bear, and as showing suppressed homosexual feeling moving towards freer expression. The Shakespeare poems – sometimes loosely interpreted – suggest kinds of feeling rather than precise content; their imagery mostly relates only indirectly to the film's visual content.

Much of the film uses a freeze-frame technique (slowed shooting and projection) which means the images appear almost as a fast-moving slide show. In some contexts the protagonists appear to move mechanically, as if not fully alive. In others the method allows the viewer to dwell on images as evidently constructed and non-naturalistic, and Jarman to dwell with a gay (or queer) eye on the physical beauty of his protagonists, from fascination with whom the film had begun. The impetus to gaze at the beauty of a young man, and – as in the Sonnets – to explore the meanings that can be found in (obsession with) male beauty, is fundamental to the cinematography. As in a dream, focus is blurred and colour unstable. Non-naturalistic effects

are re-enforced by disorientating disjunctions between image and
soundtrack – as when, in a landscape of dry rocks and swirling dust,
sounds of panting (the effort to walk) are accompanied by sounds of a
quite different impediment, the swish of wading through water. Some
repeated motifs apparently carry a symbolic charge, though how this
should be read is left for the viewer, prompted by context, to determine
– a radar dish (surveillance, antagonistic watch being kept?); a high
steel-mesh fence (excluding or imprisoning); a burning car (industrial
detritus? – set against images from nature); two chalice-like flaming
torches (love as religion?); a light-reflecting mirror flashed towards the
camera (warding off prying eyes? – though Jarman initiates will recall
the mirrors used by Dee in seeking communication with angels). The
protagonists at first carry on their shoulders literal burdens, one
a container drum, the other a cross-beam or yoke (pains of oppression,
concealment, non-reciprocation? Jarman thought of the yoke as 'the
weight of received thought' [interview in *Afterimage*, 12]).

Much of the film can be interpreted in a somewhat free way, as an
interaction between image sequences and texts in which meaning is
left for the viewer to elicit from local and total contexts. The sonnets
are used with image-sequences that divide loosely into three broad
movements – isolation (burdens, dryness, caves): 57, 90, 43, 53, 148,
126; towards release (swimming, water): 29, 94, 30, 55; love (from
wrestling to kissing): 27 and 61; coda (the lovers again separate): 56
and 104. The poems are almost exclusively from the WH sequence;
only 148 (on love's distorted judgements) is from the Dark Lady
group. Though the film is non-narrative and transitions are not
sharply distinguished, new elements enter and existing materials are
discarded (sometimes temporarily) in ways that suggest shifts of register or phases of development, and these play a part in eliciting
meaning. Local relationships are at times slight, or emphasize the
film's non-narrative nature, as when 'Then hate me when thou wilt'
(90), envisaging the desolation of desertion, is used as part of
the opening sequence, before the protagonists have met: mood is
congruent (the pain of isolation), but not situation.

Nevertheless, however the film was composed, some images are likely to strike the viewer as interacting directly with their texts, as with the opening images, which accompany a sonnet of self-abnegation, 'Being your slave, what should I do but tend / Upon the hours and times of your desire?' (57). A young man (Phillip Williamson, protagonist A) sits alone, in a room into which sunlight pours through a latticed window. Light outside throws into relief darkness inside; a ticking clock reinforces the poem's consciousness of time's painfully slow passage in the beloved's absence ('the world-without-end hour / Whilst I, my sovereign, watch the clock for you'). 'World without end', from the Prayer Book doxology: this love is a religion; the beloved is the speaker's god as well as his king. Love is complete obsession and unquestioning dependence. That is the apparent sense of the sonnet, but an alternative sense can be elicited, though it would be difficult to hear in Judi Dench's straightforward delivery. Albeit not in such a way as directly to impugn the beloved, an undercurrent of bitterness is also part of the lover's experience: beneath self-abasement flickers resentment. Pangs of disprized love seep through ambiguous terms: 'jealous' (doubtful/sexually envious), 'affairs' (business concerns/sexual liaisons). 'I have no precious time at all to spend / . . . till you require': time is precious only when the beloved's command makes it so – but the elliptical expression and delayed syntax do not sort out this sense until we have heard, as in so many of the Sonnets, that the time finally esteemed only conditionally valuable is inherently 'precious'. The lover who dares not complain or question wishes to do both. 'So true a fool is love that, in your will, / Though you do anything, he thinks no ill.' If Love thought no ill he might indeed be a fool: feeling bitterness and jealousy, and saying what he feels, albeit through apparent negations ('Nor dare I chide . . . Nor think . . . Nor question'), the lover expresses a wish to chide which is a timorous form of chiding. He is not wholly the self-abnegating 'fool' he pretends to be. By the end of the sonnet the answer to the opening apparently rhetorical question, 'What should I do?', seems less obvious. A distance has been opened up between the speaker and his apparently total devotion – a distance that retrospection shows was present from the beginning. The film's visual imagery, and Dench's straightforward delivery, appropriate the poem for a simpler purpose, to convey the lover's patient suffering in his isolation. As he turns to face the camera the film draws the viewer in: we are invited to identify with the devastating feelings to which love can give rise. But though the film simplifies and intensifies, it also powerfully conveys what the whole Sonnet sequence so often hopes it will memorialize but cannot. As the gaze of the camera invites the viewer to feel beauty's power, the film records and exhibits the beauty of a particular young man.

Two fundamental recapitulations of the opening situation – isolation (A gazing through his latticed window), and surveillance (protagonist B, Paul Reynolds, with his mirror flashed into the camera, warding off prying eyes) – are taken in new directions by 'When most I wink, then do my eyes best see' (43). The poem might appear to be for reading with a text, its paradoxes and continuous wordplay difficult to take in aurally. But the wit is not the expression of complex feelings or ideas: the verbal surface is complicated; the deep sense is simple. Dreams of the beloved seem more real than waking consciousness; only the beloved's actual presence can bestow full happiness. Whether or not the full significance of the verbal wit is understood, the pure patterning of the language – hanging on to a word repeated in some different sense or as a different part of speech – is of itself expressive. The compulsion to repeat signifies obsession: 'darkly bright . . . bright in dark . . . shadow shadows . . . shadow's form form happy show . . . unseeing eyes . . . sightless eyes': the flashing mirrors take their cue from the verbal surface. Protagonist A gazing out from his dark room, listening to the tick of passing time, conveys the deep sense: fixation on the absent object.

This introduces a sequence in bizarrely lit caves which Jarman related to 'places where analysis began'.

The dark cave where if you went under the temple, where they would put you out if you were ill. The place where the world might be put to right. A sort of ritual. The descent into darkness

– that is like Rimbaud – the descent into the other side is necessary. (*Afterimage*, 12.)

In this burning-torch or flare-lit dreamworld, with its soundtrack of
electronically distorted chant, Sonnet 53 asks the great central question, 'What is your substance?' When this sonnet is read in the full
sequence, after poems of betrayal (35–37) and infidelity (40–42), it
may be almost irresistible to understand it as concluding with irony,
invisible to WH's vanity, or deniable if necessary: 'You like none,
none you, for constant heart'. Nobody is like you for constancy – that
is, you are completely and without scruples *in*constant, the archetype
of Inconstancy as of Beauty. Here (as elsewhere) Dench reads with no
implication of less than complete conviction. Re-contextualized by
the film the poem expresses uninflected the search for a transsexual
archetype of the Beloved – Adonis-Helen, male-female, Constancy-
and-Beauty. The episode incorporates an ostentatiously weird tableau, perhaps a version of Adonis-Helen – flickering torchlight over
B's Greekly-gayly-ideal naked upper body (master-), a new young
man with a fan (-mistress), another with the flashing mirror. B battles
against a giant shadow-reflection of himself amid bursts of fire from
a huge flame-thrower. Glimpses of the illicit; (internal) psychomachia:
preludes to transition. A emerges from the caves into light.

'Oh me! What eyes hath love put in my head?' (148): appropri-
ated from the Dark Lady group, and (like 43) concerned with love's
deflections from truth, this may seem a strange choice. The poem's
'foul faults' are faults of beauty – precisely the opposite of WH's
perfection; and WH's moral faults – subject of so many Sonnets – are
not a subject of Jarman's film. Following from 'What is your substance?' it seems a retraction, taking some wholly new direction. But
if one sees Jarman as a highly partial reader – concerned exclusively
with the poem's opening question, and in effect ignoring the rest –
148 can be seen as a continuation. Each poem asks, enthralled, on
what love depends. They entertain opposite answers: on qualities
inherent in the beloved (53); on attributes bestowed – perhaps falsely

– by the lover (148). Though this is not part of Jarman's interest, the contrast and parallel between brings out the fundamental contrast and parallel between the Sonnets' two loves, both unconventional in Elizabethan terms: the Petrarchan love-object is male; the female love-object is anti-Petrarchan. But this is construction of meaning beyond anything implied by the film.

The juxtaposition of poems here is – as much as the image sequences – pointedly diverse and disorienting: directly against (the Dark Lady's) 'foul faults' (the only immediately contiguous readings in the film) Jarman places the Sonnets' last adoring address to WH, 'O thou my lovely Boy' (126), its extraordinary opening one of the most overtly homosexual professions in Shakespeare's sequence. Among many Sonnets on the transitory nature of human beauty, this is one of the most intensely conscious of how WH's loveliness, despite its apparently miraculous power in seeming to defy the operations of time, will nevertheless be subject to decay and death. Its reference to 'wretched minutes' brings this prelude-to-release section of the film to a close with a second recapitulation of the time-conscious opening images – ticking clock, and A for the last time isolated. It is a reminder of the fundamental situation of unsatisfied longing from which this sequence began, to which it has already once returned, and which is one fundamental emotional aspect of the Sonnets.

After isolation and the threatening but finally liberating under-world, sunlight and flowers introduce the most visually lyrical and in an obvious sense beautiful section of the film, a sea-shore and water sequence. The images gradually become more homoerotic: A alternately watching and swimming, the camera's gaze fixed on his physical beauty made iridescent by water and sunlight. Since the impression produced by this alternation, that A is watching himself, is reinforced by a short section later in which he gazes at his own image in the water this initiates implications of Narcissistic self-contemplation implicit in Shakespeare's opening sequence, that Jarman develops more erotically in relation to B in the film's final section. The music, which is in part responsible for making the swimming/sea-shore images so lyrically engaging, is taken from the Sea Interludes of Britten's *Peter Grimes* – music used primarily for its eerie quality and suggestion of watery open spaces, but also music written for a subject with oblique homosexual implications (inexplicable cruelty to boys that can be understood as the perpetrator's unconscious rejection of the attraction boys hold for him). As at the very beginning, A is alone, but outside, in the sun, and the accompanying poem, 'When in disgrace with fortune and men's eyes' (29), is now not of the sorrow of love but of love as the supreme cure for sorrow. Fire from the flame-thrower bursts over A (now himself an object of desire?); he holds aloft a golden ball ('thy sweet love remembered such wealth brings').

In an extended central sequence, the first in real time (not freeze-frame – though still with non-naturalistic unstable colour), and the first in which the protagonists are brought together, a young man whose largely naked body is decorated with tattoos (centrally, on his chest, a devil) is adorned with symbols suggesting royalty or power – a crown, necklace, rope of pearls (in his hand), and scimitar (in his lap). He is ritually washed by B (bells and drums accompany each laving), who repeatedly kisses him formally and gently on the chest, arms, legs, and feet, and apparently adored by A, who watches, kneeling, the flaming torches in his hands. If this is 'conversation' with an angel, it is a Blakean (or perhaps just fallen) angel-devil. As the accompanying reading of 'They that have power to hurt' (94) suggests ('moving others . . . themselves as stone, / Unmoved'), he appears indifferent to the young men of whom he might be supposed the guardian. As with the opening sequence and Sonnet 57, Jarman simplifies to intensify: the remote beloved is enthroned, served, and adored, a 'lord' to those who are 'rightly . . . stewards of [his] excellence'. This is the beloved of the framing Sonnets, 29 and 30, by whom 'all losses are restored and sorrows end'. There is nothing in the images of Sonnet 94's 'but if' turn from praise through clenched teeth that culminates in 'Lilies that fester smell far worse than weeds' – nothing of all those strands in the Sonnets which imply the corruption of WH, corruption that love wishes not to see but cannot evade.

A pouring water over his face and torso from a large mother-of-pearl shell returns to freeze-frame and the implications of the swimming sequence – water as cleansing and renewing; even, now it is poured over the head, baptizing. 'When to the sessions of sweet silent thought' (30) repeats the pattern of 'When in disgrace . . . ': a catalogue of sorrows; love as the complete antidote. 'Remembrance of things past' is embodied in a ghostly or dream-like overlay of B with flaming torches from the pre-meeting cave section. Paralleled in text and in technique, the water sequences, in which love is release and renewal, frame the extended, ritualistic presentation of the angel-devil-king, who brings the protagonists together. With caves and the firework-flare now more for imagery than symbolism ('unswept stone', 'shine more bright'), the whole movement is celebrated in one of the most confident and positive poems of the Shakespeare sequence, 'Not marble, nor the gilded monuments / Of princes, shall outlive this powerful rhyme' (55). WH will live for ever in Shakespeare's poem, as he lived in past and will live in future lovers – Shakespeare's readers, Phillip and Paul (A and B), Jarman's viewers.

The protagonists, torsos naked, wrestle, but with balletic body-handling that suggests rather affection than pugnacity. Freeze-frame drained to black and white alternates with real time and natural colour, a contrast which intensifies the effect of warm flesh, delicate touch, and intimate feeling as the wrestlers nestle together in sleep. For this climax of fulfilment the poems are unhappy. Both are about the absent beloved's longed-for presence, and how love keeps the lover from rest. 'Weary with toil, I haste me to my bed' (27) is in part positive: a vision of the beloved 'like a jewel . . . / Makes black night beauteous'; but the main effect is of restless, inappeasable obsession. 'Is it thy will thy image should keep open / My heavy eyelids?' (61) adds to this a sting in the tail: the pains of unsatisfied longing are compounded by jealous fears. In retrospect the surprise of the final line ('From me far off, with others all too near') can be seen as prepared: 'jealousy', though indeed a cause of wakefulness, is not, as postulated, the addressee's; the speaker's 'true love' contrasts with the youth's; 'wake' has meanings both creditable to WH ('lie watchful') and opprobrious ('stay up partying'). For Jarman the poems were perhaps predominantly expressions of unsatisfied longing and unrest – counterpoints to the images. In the film the beloved is present, not an 'imaginary sight', so the effect is reversed: for 'no quiet', rest. Or Jarman may have expected the viewer to hear the poems only as about love and sleep. In a climax of chastely homoerotic pleasure, with images of a Caravaggesque youth interposed, and after a final warding-off of prying eyes by the mirror shone straight into the camera, to an unusually lyrical string accompaniment the protagonists kiss gently, on the hands, chest, and lips. But Jarman adds his own bitter twist, not jealousy but Narcissism. In what is perhaps presented as B's dream (he sleeps, watched by A) images three times interposed show him – eyes closed, still apparently in sleep – approach his own image in a mirror as though approaching the face of a lover, lips parted in an expression of sensual arousal. At the third appearance he kisses his mirror image. The obvious significance is to imply that B's engagement with A is Narcissistic – a suggestion Jarman might be understood as taking from the Sonnets, though he uses none of the poems that carry this implication, which is at its strongest in the early sequence on WH's damaging self-love. 'Is it thy will' confuses lover and beloved, though not in this way; but as an adaptive reader Jarman may well have read 'It is my love that keeps mine eye awake' as implying what in context it does not (Shakespeare: 'My own true love'; Jarman: 'My own self-love'). Whether or not Jarman saw the source of this as in Shakespeare, the sequence is a striking dissonance in what is otherwise, for all its unusual cinematic aspects, a broadly straightforward narrative of reciprocal gay love.

In the closing sequence the radar dish returns, though almost obliterated by flowers (love overcomes surveillance?). Finally B buries his face in a hanging stalk of blossom (love is at one with natural beauty?). But everything is perhaps presented as in memory: A gazes at B as he lies asleep while a collage of fragments partly re-edited from material used earlier recalls what brought them to this condition – A in the caves and swimming, B with the flaming torches. Even new material is related to what went before – A in the gardens of the Elizabethan House (not now looking out on them), the fan signifying his femininity. Finally A and B are brought together in characteristic activities – A swimming projected simultaneously with B among blossom. The accompanying poems are a parallel mixture of conviction and uncertainty. 'Sweet love, renew thy force' (56): the speaker may be urging himself not to let love slacken; but if 'Sweet love' is taken as an address the slackening stems from the beloved. As it becomes clear that the slackening of love is caused by absence ('this sad interim') the poem acknowledges that this might equally have been a cause of intensification. The ambiguity of 'return of love' (reappearance of the beloved/reciprocation of the feeling of love) maintains the doubt about whose love requires a spur. 'To me, fair friend, you never can be old' (104) expresses a parallel uncertainty: does beauty remain an attribute of the beloved, or is it attributed to him by the speaker's refusal to see change that has taken place? 'Ere you were born was beauty's summer dead': this affirmation of the beloved's supreme beauty acknowledges the subjective nature of the perception from which the poem is built – what (it seemed) 'never can be old' will in time be dead. B burying his face in blossom is beauty's summer. But A gazing at B while he slept – dreaming, it appeared, of kissing his alter ego; A alone in the grand house's garden not far from where he began – with his fan, boy-girl outsider: these are reminders within the final sequences of the film of the melancholy that is an undertone to all but a few of the poems.

Love between attractive young men, obviously compatible in age, appearance, and style, breaks through barriers. Though the film is so experimental in technique, and experimental in the ways in which it elicits meaning from sequences of images in relation to each other and to texts, music, and other sound effects, it is finally relatively conventional in its account of sex, desire, and love between men, and sex, desire, and love in the Shakespeare Sonnets. The missing issue, which transforms everything, is age. At the date of the setting of *Protagoras*, Alcibiades, then ideally beautiful, was seventeen, Socrates approaching forty. When he met the teenage Tommaso Michelangelo was fifty-seven. Mann's Aschenbach is over fifty, Tadzio fourteen. Whatever the situation lying behind Shakespeare's Sonnets may or may not have been, a similar gap in age is implied between the sweet and lovely boy addressed (108, 126) and the speaker, 'beated and chopped with tanned antiquity' (62), 'with time's injurious hand crushed and o'erworn' (63), whose age suggests winter, night, a death-bed (73). Shakespeare's hyper-romantic Troilus may not be alone in finding in all love a gap between desire that is boundless and fulfil-ment that is 'slave to limit'. But the often melancholy awareness of an abyss that love can scarcely hope to transcend, in this precise form of all that is implied by a gulf between youth and age, is a defining aspect of love in the WH Sonnets. In leaving this out, despite Jarman's insistence on 'queer' *The Angelic Conversation* is a gay film.

But its implied way of reading is exemplary. 'Ein Kunstwerk könne dem Beschauer recht liebe werden wenn es ihn zwänge nach eigener Sinnesweise es sich auszulegen' (a work of art can only become truly loved by the beholder if it forces him to interpret it according to his own way of thinking: Goethe, in conversation, reported by Friedrich von Müller). This will always be less than the full range of a great work's possibilities, but that is the way a selection of those possibili-ties becomes real to a particular reader. 'I seek . . . to bring you, reader [viewer], into the atmosphere of the theme or thought – there to pursue your own flight'. This is what Jarman does with Shakespeare. *The Angelic Conversation* 'does not dictate . . . [it] allows the mind to draw its own conclusions' – by exploring, that is, in an engaged and creative way Shakespeare's poems and Jarman's images, and thinking about the kinds of meaning each opens up in the other. Since mean-ing in the film has no appearance of being circumscribed, the proc-esses of constructing understanding very obviously open the poems to readings that draw on interaction with the experiences and ideas the reader-viewer brings.

It is exemplary for the reader's relation to all reading.

Text Note

1. See, for example, William Empson, 'Shakespeare's Angel,' *New Statesman*, October 1963, 447–48; Stephen Orgel, *Impersonations: The Performance of Gender in Shakespeare's England*, Cambridge: Cambridge University Press, 1996, pp. 56–57; Alan Sinfield, 'Coming on to Shakespeare: Off-stage Action and Sonnet 20', *Shakespeare*, 3 (2007), 108–25; and most elaborately Joseph Pequigney, *Such is My Love: A Study of Shakespeare's Sonnets*, Chicago: University of Chicago Press, 1985, chapter 3.

Dwelling in the Words: Reading the Sonnets Aloud

If [people] are to read poetry at all, if they are to enjoy beautiful rhythm, if they are to get from poetry anything but what it has in common with prose, they must hear it spoken by men who have music in their voices and a learned understanding of its sound. There is no poem so great that a fine speaker cannot make it greater or that a bad ear cannot make it nothing.

(W. B. Yeats, 'Samhain: 1906. Literature and the Living Voice')

In poetry you must love the words, the ideas and the images and rhythms with all your capacity to love anything at all.

(Wallace Stevens, 'Adagia', *Opus Posthumous*)

Reading aloud is one of the best ways of fully inhabiting the experience of a poem – participating in its feelings, taking pleasure in its words. The 'learned understanding' of which Yeats speaks is the ability to give aural shape to the structures of verse, formal and syntactic, so as to bring out their beauty and expressivity – just as imagining poetry in these terms in the mind's ear is fundamental to the pleasures of silent reading.

Poetry can be a private art. Reading poetry often means a silent reader alone with a book. Shakespeare's Sonnets do not imply the same reading expectations as *Beowulf*. But what the silent reader does (or should do) is imagine the sound-scapes of a poem as they would be if the poem were read aloud. And silent reading often requires the complement of reading aloud. The physical voice, like the face, is both given and developed – an aural (as the face is a visual) repository of one's emotional and intellectual identity. Reading or speaking out loud is a test of the depth and sincerity of one's engagement with any words, for a priest as for a politician, for a lover as for a liar. Poetry is a special case only because full engagement requires a practised understanding of its structures.

Sound in poetry is intrinsic to meaning. Meaning in poetry is never wholly independent of sound. It is because sound is so important in poetry that poets of very different types – poets who are stylized and musical, poets who are colloquial and prosaic – have affirmed the importance of reading poetry aloud, from Wordsworth, to Hopkins, to Auden, to Bunting.

[Wordsworth] I require nothing more than an animated or impassioned recitation, adapted to the subject. Poems, however humble in their kind, if they be good in that kind, cannot read themselves.

(Preface, *Poems of 1815*)

[Hopkins] Remember what applies to all my verse, that it is, as living art should be, made for performance, and that its performance is not reading with the eye but loud, leisurely, poetical (not rhetorical) recitation, with long rests, long dwells on the rhyme and other marked syllables, and so on. This sonnet ['Spelt from Sibyl's Leaves'] should be almost sung: it is most carefully timed in *tempo rubato*.

(Letter, 11 December, 1886)

[Auden] Poetry must move our emotions, or excite our intellect . . . and the stimulus is the audible spoken word and cadence, to which in all its power of suggestion and incantation we must surrender, as we do when talking to an intimate friend. . . . No poetry . . . which when mastered is not better heard than read is good poetry.

(Introduction, *The Poet's Tongue*, 1935)

[Bunting] Poetry, like music, is to be heard. . . . Poetry lies dead on the page, until some voice brings it to life, just as music, on the stave, is no more than instructions to the player. A skilled musician can imagine the sound, more or less, and a skilled reader can try to hear, mentally, what his eyes see in print; but nothing will satisfy either of them till his ears hear it as real sound in the air. Poetry must be read aloud.

('A Statement', *Descant on Rawthey's Madrigal*, 1968)

'Animated or impassioned recitation'; a 'living art . . . made for performance'; surrender to the 'spoken word and cadence . . . in all its power of suggestion and incantation'. Though such various poets agree however, on the importance of performance, and though the performance of poetry was a subject of ancient literary criticism and education, modern criticism has fought shy of it. But the reader who does not understand a poem's aural shapes knows only a shadow of its living reality. An ability to perform, at least to the mind's ear, is – or should be – basic to every other kind of critical activity.

Any aspect of the sound of poetry can be expressive, including, for special effects, the music of vowels and consonants, in patterns of rhyme, assonance, and alliteration. But the main musical effects of poetry do not depend on this. If they did the music of Shakespeare's poetry would be almost as lost as the music of Virgil's. If you think, as Basil Bunting claimed, that the music of poetry consists in 'the tone relations of vowels, the relations of consonants to one another, which are like instrumental colour in music' ('A Statement'), then you cannot be confident that you are hearing the music of any poetry written much more than a century ago as the poet or the first audience heard it: such music as you find you must take as a mixture of your own creation and the gift of chance. Between Shakespeare's sixteenth-century Warwickshire and the mellifluous received pronunciation of Sir John Gielgud there is a great gulf fixed; and its precise contours cannot be known. The music of poetry depends not on those aspects of the sound of language that differ from one system of pronunciation to another but on those that are broadly constant. Above all the music of poetry depends on the sounds of the shapes of syntax (speech) interacting with the sounds of the shapes of form (song). This means an expressive interaction of different modes or structurations of language – prose or colloquial syntax cutting across the formal shapes of verse, speech rhythms interacting with metrical patterns. In discussing the sounds and rhythms of poetry there is no avoiding detail about its structure. This need not be unmitigated dry biscuit so long as one keeps in view the aims – enjoyment of beauty, participation in feeling, by dwelling in the words.

Understanding structure should come as easily as it can: some ears are more readily tuned than others. Rhythm and metrical pattern, and the delicate and variable ways in which they function, are fundamental to heightened consciousness and passionate expression in poetry. They also seem to be among the most difficult aspects of poetry fully to actualize. Hearing and feeling the rhythm of a poem is an art, not a science. There is never a single way of hearing a poem's rhythms: competent readers will often disagree about their aural realization. As T. S. Eliot has it (on his own reading of *Four Quartets*), 'A poem . . . of any depth and complexity . . . should be capable of being read in many ways, and with a variety of emotional emphases. . . . The chief value of the author's record is as a guide to the rhythms'; but 'another reader, reciting the poem, need not feel bound to reproduce these rhythms' (sleeve note to HMV CLP 1115). As with other aspects of criticism, alternative interpretations are always possible, and will usually relate to everything else – from the primary sense or feeling of a poem to judgements about audience and context. In realizing rhythms the reader listens for and aims to recreate a musical quality, but not one that corresponds to the regular beat of Western music. The rhythms of poetry are more free and irregular. Freedom and irregularity are essential to their nature as vehicles of heightened feeling – as is the underlying pulse, the beat from which they vary.

Stress is irregular in periodicity and in degree; and it is relative, not absolute. Words can assume a degree of stress when part of a metrical pattern that they would not bear in prose, where no pattern has been established. The rhythms of poetry are tendencies and relativities: the usual notation (stressed and unstressed syllables) is, and can only be, a rough guide. In poetry rhythm is not like a mechanism (a clock, a metronome): it is like the heartbeat, the pulse, the breathing – a bodily, human measure, responsive to feeling, subject to variation in periodicity and in force.

A properly rhythmical reading will come naturally once the ear is attuned to the basic metre, and will negotiate between that underlying metrical structure, the natural rhythms of speech, and the requirements of meaning. It should not slavishly follow the metre in violation of ordinary speech rhythms or the demands of emphasis required by the sense, nor should it follow the demands of sense or ordinary speech rhythms in such a way as wholly to lose track of the metre. As Coleridge put it (praising an actress 'who pronounced the blank verse of Shakespeare . . . better than I ever heard it pronounced'), 'she hit the exact medium between the obtrusive iambic march of recitation, and . . . convert[ing] the language into a sort of prose intolerable to a good ear' (letter to Byron, 15 October 1815). No thumping metric, no flattening to prose: the constant, subtle presence of a variable pulse.

When Yeats recorded some of his poems for a BBC broadcast in 1932 he announced:

> I am going to read my poems with great emphasis upon their rhythm, and that may seem strange if you are not used to it. I remember the great English poet, William Morris, coming in a rage out of some lecture hall where somebody had recited a passage out of his *Sigurd the Volsung*. 'It gave me a devil of a lot of trouble,' said Morris, 'to get that thing into verse.' It gave *me* a devil of a lot of trouble to get into verse the poems that I am going to read, and that is why I will not read them as if they were prose.
>
> (British Library, Sound Archive, recording reference 2LP0033699/1LP0054633)

He did indeed then read 'The Fiddler of Dooney' with great emphasis on its rhythm, and with his rich Anglo-Irish lilt showing at least one meaning of 'music in the voice'. But 'The Fiddler of Dooney' is a ballad: it is written in an emphatic metre. Yeats did not read the meditative 'The Lake Isle of Innisfree' with the same rhythmic emphasis. The rhythm of *The Ancient Mariner* suggests a quite different mode of reading from the rhythm of 'Frost at Midnight'. And even within the relatively unified styles of the Sonnets, 'That time of year thou mayst in me behold' (73), in which rhythmic smoothness works with the rhetorical structure of parallel quatrains to suggest meditative repose, invites a quite different reading manner from 'Th'expense of spirit in a waste of shame' (129), in which rhythmic irregularity works with the rhetorical structure of parallels and antitheses crushed close together to suggest emotional perturbation.

When different ways of reading rhythms present themselves – following the colloquial stress or the metrical accentuation – whichever you chose, you are likely to retain a mental impression of the alternative possibility which will influence the feeling of the lines, though probably this cannot be made more than subliminally audible in aural delivery. How best to negotiate between the metrical expectation and the natural spoken emphasis where the two conflict depends on the degree of stylization of the poem and the reader's own feeling about how he or she can most expressively project the words.

The metre of Shakespeare's Sonnets – and the dominant metre of English poetry from the sixteenth to the twentieth century – is a five-beat line alternating unstressed and stressed syllables (iambic pentameter). If a reader's ear is attuned to anything it is attuned to this. But also native to English poetry is a fundamentally different kind of metrical pattern – a four-stressed alliterative line in which there is no regular alternation of stressed and unstressed syllables. This, the rhythm of Old English poetry, was still used by contemporaries of Chaucer, and has been revived by some modern and contemporary poets. English seems to be almost as naturally attuned to a four- as to a five-beat line, and iambic pentameter has a tendency to collapse into a four-beat structure. This happens because stress is dependent both on pattern and on sense, and, unless there is a deliberate aim to make them so, these are seldom identical. While words in a metrical structure may bear some stress against the requirements of sense in order to sustain a feeling of pattern, such words usually bear a lesser stress than sense words. 'To be, or not to be; that is the question'. The structure of iambic pentameter requires a feeling of residual stress on the second 'be', but the sense does not. A competent actor will give the line four, not five, main stresses:

     /   /   /   /
To be, or not to be; that is the question.

This freedom is common in Shakespeare. 'Unthrifty loveliness, why dost thou spend . . . ' (x/x/xx/xx/: Sonnet 4). So is freedom in the opposite direction: 'Savage, extreme, rude, cruel, not to trust' can scarcely be read naturally without six beats (/xx///x/x/: Sonnet 129). Actually to read Shakespeare's iambic pentameter as though every line contains five stresses would mean emphasizing syllables that will not bear stress without distortion, or passing over syllables that invite a natural stress. Reading should both maintain a sense of underlying pattern and recognize that the structure is not a metrical bed of Procrustes in which every consideration gives way to regular recurrence. Shakespeare did not aim for the kinds of smoothness cultivated by poets like Pope or Tennyson. Rhythm in the Sonnets can tend towards the colloquial ('When in disgrace with fortune and men's eyes': /xx/x/xx//, 29); or can be expressively rough ('Let me not to the marriage of true minds / Admit impediments: love is not love . . . ': /x/xx/xx// / x/x/xx/xx/, 116) – though this is mild compared with the ruggedness of Donne, who often counterpoints metrical regularity with rhythms imitating those of speech, and whom smoothly classical Ben Jonson thought 'for not keeping of accent deserved hanging' (Conversations with William Drummond). Compared with this, the Rival Poet sonnets (78–86) show Shakespeare aware of writing in a lyric mode that could be seen as conservative.

Like rhythm, syntax too may run – beautifully and expressively – counter to the requirements of making the simplicities of metrical pattern audible. In most poetry grammatical structure is not conterminous with the line, and some of the energy of the verse comes from an interplay between syntax and form, so it is important not to lose the feeling of either. The reader has to guide the listener's ear through the grammatical structure; but, with that primary desideratum, has also to consider how to bring out the formal shapes. This form-syntax interaction will vary with the style of the poem: line endings, for example, are heard more readily when they are marked by rhyme – as they always are in Shakespeare's Sonnets – but they should not be over-marked. The line ending, like a bar line in music, is a way of showing the rhythmic structure; but except in some nursery rhyme rhythms ('Ding dong bell. / Pussy's in the well') the line-ending is not itself an element in the rhythmic structure. It no more requires a break than every bar-line requires an accent. On the contrary, interrupting the syntax should not be used as a crutch to make metrical structure audible. And line-endings are not like bar-lines other than as visual markers of structure, because in the rhythms of poetry there is no equivalent of regularly spaced beats in a bar. Rhythmical recurrence is part of the heightening of poetry as passionate speech, but over-formalised it acts not as an aid to expressing feeling but a barrier to it – makes rigid what should be fluid. The reader needs to embody aurally both syntax and form, not one at the expense of the other.

Intonation helps to point syntax. It may also decide implications of sense. Different ways of saying the same phrase or sentence may be acceptable as normal English intonation, though one may express better than another the appropriate sense in a given context. Intonation functions in part simply as a guide to the syntax – which is especially important when the syntax is complex. It is also an instrument of interpretation. So long as reading maintains the underlying formal pattern against which the syntax is in revolt, tension between the demands of form and syntax can strongly enforce a feeling of passionate utterance by giving a sense of energy both contained and bursting out. 'Then hate me when thou wilt, if ever, now, / Now, . . .' (90) – though such syntax of colloquial utterance is rare in the Sonnets, and in the Sonnets Shakespeare does not counterpoint syntax against form in the extreme ways found in Donne or Milton.

Simpler than rhythm and syntax is pace. As with everything about reading aloud, there are no general rules. But people often read too quickly. The expressive effects of sound cannot be heard if the reader rushes. Dwelling in the words means that a reader must convey a sense that he or she is taking enough time to take pleasure in them in all their aspects as structured sounds and enough time to think and feel their meanings. Beyond that, everything depends on the poem and the actual or assumed audience. A poem of action (narrative) can often be read more quickly that a poem of meditation (lyric). Poetry of argument and the spoken voice (Browning) may require more variation than poetry of song (Tennyson). It is indicative for pace and tone in performance of the Sonnets that, in poetry that so notably exploits effects of verbal music, Shakespeare draws analogies with song (Sonnets 100, 105). But all poetry requires variation related to overall sense and form and immediate syntax and rhythm, and variation to emphasize central issues or to mark changes of direction. Pace may vary more in dramatic than in non-dramatic poetry, because in dramatic poetry (narrative, as well as for the stage) there is more need to accommodate the inflections of a (supposed) speaking voice. But always there should be the feeling of underlying regularity – as Hopkins has it, like *tempo rubato* in music: the player maintains connection with the basic pulse while, for expressive purposes, but within limits, varying the pace.

Many of the Sonnets benefit from lyrically meditative, slow delivery, but a reader cannot always draw out patterns of sound without affectation. So long as he or she is enjoying sound patterns in the mouth and in the ear they will have their effect without undue emphasis. As Ted Hughes has it, sound pattern in poetry 'roots itself directly in the nerves of the ear' (*By Heart*, Introduction). Response can be physical before it is mental. 'When to the sessions of sweet silent thought' (30) is typical of how verbal music works in the Sonnets, sometimes with reference to sense, but also as pure pleasure in sound and shape. While this creates meaning in a general way by reinforcing feeling, it does so without reference to precise sense.

> When . . . sessions . . . sweet silent . . .
>> . . . summon . . .
>> . . . sigh . . .
>> . . . old woes new wail . . . waste
>
> Then . . .
>> . . . death's dateless . . .
>> And weep . . .
>> And moan . . .
>
> Then . . . grieve at grievances . . .
>> . . . woe to woe . . .
>> . . . fore-bemoaned moan . . .
>> . . . new pay . . . not paid . . .

When the main sound and structure words are isolated like this it should be obvious what Auden means about surrendering to the 'spoken word and cadence . . . in all its power of suggestion'; what Hopkins suggests by 'long rests, long dwells on . . . marked syllables': patterns of sound that can be vocalized in the line, in the quatrain, in the sonnet as a whole. T. S. Eliot complained of Milton that you need to read his poetry twice, once for the sense and once for the music ('Milton', 1936). Whether or not Eliot identified a special problem of Milton's verse, he surely identified a general difficulty about reading poetry. Precision of meaning, play of imagination, richness of music: reading should aim for all these, but they cannot always all interact, or even fully co-exist. We may read the same poem in different ways for different pleasures.

We may also read the same poem in different ways for different meanings. When a poem is fundamentally and finally ambivalent

('They that have power to hurt' [94]), that can usually be conveyed in a single voicing. When a poem has a surface meaning (loving, sentiment-full) and an undercurrent (bitter, resentful) which perhaps only reveals itself on subsequent readings ('Take all my loves, my love' [40]) probably both tones cannot be present simultaneously in a single vocalisation. Not every critical account can be embodied in an aural realization – though every aural realization has critical implications.

It is with a view to realizing the importance of sound in poetry that Wallace Stevens discusses responses in different historical periods and cultural situations to what he calls 'nobility' ('The Noble Rider and the Sounds of Words'). Stevens admits that 'nobility' is a gestural term, a quality of 'intelligence and desire for life' that 'resolves itself into a number of vibrations, movements, changes' but cannot be named. (It can be shown by instances, one of which, for Stevens, is Shakespeare's Sonnet 'Since brass, nor stone, nor earth, nor boundless sea' [65].) Nobility in this sense, Stevens claims, inheres in the sound of words in poetry. Stevens makes a point of not tying down his meaning; the account is not a statement but a search. But for those who have ears to hear, in poetry nobility ('intelligence, desire for life') is to be listened for in discipline of structure (every aspect of formal shaping) combined with precision and intensity of language at once denotative and connotative, semantic (with resonances etymological, historical, cultural) and musical. This 'makes us listen to words . . . loving them and feeling them, makes us search the sound of them, for a finality, a perfection . . . which it is only within the power of the acutest poet to give them'. With pure music one can say a great deal about why a piece is satisfying, but this will never be a full account of what the music means. With poetry one can go further with meaning, but this may deflect the intellect from listening for what Stevens cannot name. We can listen to all the sound effects for which the arts of verse and rhetoric have terms, but it is only when we admit that, as with music, what can be heard exceeds formulation that the craving to explain gives place to the desire to take pleasure – what Susan Sontag calls an aesthetic 'erotics'.

The sounds of rhythm and syntax, and pace. A reader has also to think about how to use his or her voice. The problem is to use the voice in such a way as to recognize the forms of art while also using the voice naturally, as it is used in the rest of life, as it aurally embodies characteristics of the individual's thinking and feeling. This is key to connecting the poet's words with the reader's own emotional and intellectual life. Without this you cannot engage with a poem with full seriousness. Many people cannot do this readily because a poem is a shaped object. The difficulty is to find ways of using one's natural voice to co-operate with and project that: to relate one's natural voice to the degree of stylization of the poem; and to find some version of the full range of one's voice that can co-operate with the characteristic 'voice' of the poet – including whatever dramatic voices the poet may create. People often read with a narrower range of intonation and expressive inflection than they use in speaking, because in reading they cut down the range of variation (pitch, stress, pace) by which they are accustomed to express themselves in speech. On the other hand, there are usual 'actorly' mistakes: treating a poem as an opportunity to display a self-consciously 'beautiful' voice, or supposing that poetry requires a voice infused with emotion. On the contrary, the voice is a vehicle: it should not draw attention to itself. The reader should not displace attention from the words by spicing them up with artificial additives. As T. S. Eliot puts it, 'So far as possible, the reciter should not dramatize. It is the words that matter, not the feeling about them' ('T. S. Eliot answers questions'). Eliot is here discussing poetry that is philosophical or meditative. In his own reading of *The Waste Land* he made more concessions to the praise of Dickens's Sloppy (*Our Mutual Friend*) that he had once intended as a title for that many-voiced poem: 'he do the police in different voices'. Even at his most austere Eliot's practice as a reader shows he did not mean that a performer should read colourlessly; rather that the reader should trust the words, giving what Wordsworth calls an 'animated' realization of their formal and metrical arrangement. Reading should reveal the expressivity the poet has found in the language and built into its organization, not apply expressivity from outside. There may be a great deal of colour present, but it should be the colours of the poem's words interacting with the colours of the reader's personality.

To do this fully the reader has to live with a poem. Part of that 'living with' is to read the poem repeatedly, working it into one's own voice, interiorizing a sense of its feelings and ideas. The poet Charles Tomlinson has remarked that reading aloud is 'a way of life' – meaning that to read poetry aloud with full, natural expressivity may require being accustomed to reading aloud in a variety of situations, intimate and formal, from bed-time story to lectern.

From this point of view the advice of the great French poet Paul Valéry may at first appear – as I once thought it – the epitome of error.

> In studying a piece of poetry to be spoken aloud, one should never take as a beginning or point of departure ordinary discourse or current speech, and then rise from the level of prose to the desired poetic tone; on the contrary, I believe one should start from song, put oneself in the attitude of the singer, tune one's voice to the fullness of musical sound, and from that point descend to the slightly less vibrant state suitable to verse. It seemed to me that this was the only way to preserve the musical essence of poems. . . . The first condition for speaking verse well is an understanding of what it is not, and of how great a difference separates it from ordinary language. . . .
>
> We note that in song the words tend to lose their importance as meaning, that they do most frequently lose it, whereas at the other extreme, in everyday prose, it is the musical value that tends to disappear; so much so that song on the one side and prose on the other are placed, as it were, symmetrically in relation to verse, which holds an admirable and very delicate balance between the sensual and intellectual forces of language. . . .

Above all, do not be in a hurry to reach the meaning. Approach it without forcing and, as it were, imperceptibly. Attain the tenderness and the violence only by the music and through it. . . . Remain in this purely musical state until the moment the meaning, having gradually supervened, can no longer mar the musical form. You will gradually introduce it as the supreme nuance which will transfigure your piece without altering it.

('On Speaking Verse')

Valéry's advice (it goes without saying) is not English. More than that, it draws on French traditions of writing and performance that are markedly different from the English. W. H. Auden wittily remarked that playing Racine is more like singing Wagner than acting Shakespeare, and that French classical tragedy is 'opera for the unmusical' ('Writing', *The Dyer's Hand*). The relation of much English poetry to spoken English – of Shakespeare's poetry, even in the relative smoothness of the Sonnets – is closer than the relation of the classic tradition of French poetry to spoken French. With English poetry the view of Thomas Gray – 'the language of the age is never the language of poetry' (Letter, 8 April 1742) – has been aberrant. Wordsworth's account – 'a selection of the language really spoken by men' (Preface to *Lyrical Ballads*) – indicates the relation of poetic to spoken language to which English poetry has constantly returned. The way in which English poetry should be read – with a feeling for all the resources of the language as spoken – follows from that.

But there must also be 'selection', and Valéry's sense of poetry as holding a 'delicate balance between the sensual and intellectual forces of language' is quite as valid for English poetry as for French. In bringing together the mind (language) and the body (vocal tone), voice is ideally placed to be the vehicle of this complementarity: meaning and feeling – but it must be the whole voice. Discussing reading aloud with students on some occasion I produced the doctrine from Eliot about the reciter not dramatizing. After expressions of astonishment, and polite but not entirely contained amusement, they asked if I supposed that in reading aloud I did not dramatize. Naturally taken aback, I conceded that there might be more than one view; that one cannot fully recognize what one does; that it is important, just as a grand dictionary shows meanings by definitions and by examples of usage, to have principles complemented by exemplification. Though I also concluded that, while I may not have represented adequately what I wanted – using a version of my own speaking voice, not applying colour from outside, and so on – if you do use the real range of your voice, not just the range usually thought acceptable for polite conversation, the result might appear not *un*dramatized. But I have since come to think that one should go further to accommodate the apparently French desiderata of Valéry about the music of poetry.

In verse drama, Yeats affirms ('Lapis Lazuli'), actors who understand their art 'do not break up their lines to weep' – nor for any other purpose. So it is in reading all verse: the reader must find expressiveness, not in naturalistic effects at odds with form, but in a full realization of the complementary effects of the spoken voice and the music of formal organization. It is in bringing out this complementarity – the voice of natural feeling; the aural realization of poetic form – that Valéry's view of the reader as a kind of singer points to a real need; but 'as a kind of singer' because singing no more gives the right idea than speaking. It suggests too deliberate and complete a break with speech. There is not an English word for the vocal tones that, without singing, go beyond speaking. But as soon as you hear a reader who has no sense of reaching up, of rising above, the idea if not precisely of 'singing' then of 'song' may suggest what is lacking: range, colour, exuberance; a proper excess; a response adequate to the otherness of the shaped object. Without this the heightened intensity that poetic form embodies will be pulled back towards prose. Only for English poetry Valéry's view might be reversed: find the natural voice; then, without ever losing that, rise towards the level of song.

This may be difficult for ears accustomed to the assumptions of naturalism – accustomed to prose as the verbal medium for all purposes, theatre as television, and an audience that is domestic with no living relation to performers. Accommodating poetry aurally to these conventions drags it towards prose, misses the experience of an audience-community (however small) interacting through shared response to heightened experience, and it undermines the characteristic thrill of the aesthetic – transcending the everyday self. This is not an issue about art and elites. Consider the Italian opera audience that cannot resist (somewhat under its breath) joining in the great Verdi choruses. It is an issue about renewing a living feeling for non-naturalistic conventions.

And, with a difference of focus, Valéry's is the advice of English-language poets too. Yeats requires not only a learned understanding of the sounds of poetry but also 'music in the voice'. Hopkins, as he envisages a meditative privacy ('poetical (not rhetorical) recitation'), requires that poetry be 'almost sung', and draws an analogy with musical performance ('in *tempo rubato*'). Auden, as he stresses the most intimate kind of speaking ('as when talking to a friend'), complements this with the 'cadence [of] . . . incantation'. Bunting's analogy for reading a poem is performing a musical score. Eliot, despite his severe advice against the actorly ('should not dramatize'), goes even further with music. In poetry he stressed the importance of 'beauty of incantation' (*The Rock*, Chorus IX). Asked about his instinct in the performance of poetry to chant, he replied: 'for me the incantatory element is very important. . . . When I read poetry myself I put myself in a kind of trance and move in rhythm to the rhythm of the piece in question' ('T. S. Eliot answers questions'). Though wary of the actorly, in reading this poet-singer-shaman ('in a kind of trance'), also (as it were) danced. It is not only through the voice that the sounds of poetry can engage the whole being.

The effect of a more incantatory intonation is to emphasize formal structure. Since the main vocal indicator of syntax is pitch, it may often do this at the expense of bringing out the syntax. It adds to the intensity of effect by emphasizing more strongly pattern, but it is also more impersonal, or at least less strongly personal. However sharply individual the tone of a particular voice may be, an incantatory tendency in reading reduces the inflections that are so important a part of what characterizes the individual speaking voice. In a liturgical context chant is music's equivalent of the priest's robes: the individual is absorbed into the office, whether of priest or cantor. Incantation is the robe of the voice. For those kinds of poetry in which (as for those kinds of reader for whom) difficulties of sense-making divert attention towards a single channel of significance – paraphrasable content – allowing oneself to receive a poem in terms of its structures of sound releases attention to a crucial aspect of poetry's full meaning. Reading aloud can re-direct attention to meaning in terms of feeling (Valéry's 'the tenderness, the violence'): inhabiting vocally the structures of a poem – syntactic and formal; its structure as speech and its structure as song – can be a non-analytic route to finding the sense. If you approach the meaning of a poem through its music, [Valéry] 'you will gradually introduce [the meaning] as the supreme nuance which will transfigure your piece without altering it'.

While an incantatory mode of performance may reduce the sense of an idiosyncratic individual voice, a style which, while remaining speech incorporates song, in drawing more resonantly on the whole vocal mechanism, may also give a heightened sense of full human thinking-and-feeling presence in the voice.

This way of reading English poetry is not out of line with the French-beyond-Valéry doctrines of Mallarmé – that in poetry language becomes a kind of musical magic: cast free of denotative senses, in poetry words work partly in terms of pure sound. But one need not accept a Mallarméan irrationalist view of poetry to agree with the slogan of Verlaine, 'la musique avant toute chose' ('Art poétique'). It is an injunction that many poets accept. Ezra Pound expands, at first tentatively, finally with his usual emphasis: 'The proportion or quality of the music [in poetry] may, and does, vary; but poetry withers and 'dries out' when it leaves music, or at least imagined music, too far behind it. . . . Poetry must be read as music and not as oratory. . . . Poets who do not study music are defective' ('Vers libre and Arnold Dolmetch'). On this view poetry so prominently avails itself of musical resources because (Eliot again) 'the poet is occupied with frontiers of consciousness beyond which words fail, though meanings still exist'; because poetry deals with 'feeling which we can only detect, so to speak, out of the corner of the eye and can never completely focus' ('The Music of Poetry'). In poetry we therefore 'touch the border of those feelings which only music can express' ('Poetry and Drama'). To approach frontiers of consciousness the poet engages the 'auditory imagination', that is, 'the feeling for syllable and rhythm, penetrating far below the conscious levels of thought and feeling' ('Matthew Arnold', *The Use of Poetry and the Use of Criticism*).[1] Ted Hughes develops the argument with a different emphasis on the kind of meaning that can be heard in the sounds of poetry: 'In our own language verbal sounds are organically linked to the vast system of root-meanings and related associations, deep in the subsoil of psychological life, beyond our immediate awareness or conscious manipulation. It is the distinction of poetry to create strong patterns in these hidden meanings as well as in the clearly audible sounds. The hidden patterns are, if anything, much the stronger. The audial memory picks up these patterns in the depths from what it hears at the surface' (*By Heart*, Introduction). Attempting to express the all but inexpressible, poetry aspires to the condition of music. The performance of poetry must recognize this.

Eliot was explicit about analogies between poetry and music: verbal music is local – rhythm, rhyme, assonance, alliteration, rhetorical balance and parallelism: the kinds of effects that Shakespeare so copiously exploits in the Sonnets. Verbal music is also structural, 'a question of the whole poem'. 'A poem . . . has a musical pattern of sound and a musical pattern of the secondary meanings of the words which compose it, and . . . these two patterns are indissoluble and one' ('The Music of Poetry') – or, as he expressed it in poetry, 'Only by the form, the pattern, / Can words or music reach / The stillness' (*Burnt Norton*, V). By 'secondary meanings' Eliot means all the ways in which words signify apart from semantically – the history of their meanings, the contextual flavours they carry, their sound qualities, and how these interact with (to adopt a musical term) the overtones of other words in the line, the stanza, the paragraph, and ultimately the poem or sequence of poems as a whole. Sound local and structural constitutes a poem's 'music'. Reading aloud gives this aural embodiment. Valéry summarized, stressing both sides of the speaking-singing complementarity, in his 'Letter to Madame C' (Claire Croiza, a singer with whom he conducted speech-song experiments performing Ronsard): 'Poetry is not music; still less is it speech. . . . One might say that it is about to sing, rather than that it sings; and that it is about to speak, rather than that it speaks'.

Some poets are, of course, nearer the singing, some nearer the speaking voice. Compare musical forms (villanelle, aubade, sestina) or poets who co-operate with their formal structures (Spenser, Tennyson) with looser verse forms (Blake in his long-line poems, Whitman) or poets with whom energy comes from over-spilling the line and from interplay between metrical and spoken accentuation (Donne, Browning). Or consider poets who choose words for their sound as much as for their sense – poets of the Old and Middle English alliterative tradition (pre-print, oral; *Beowulf*, Langland, the *Gawain*-poet), or poets such as Hopkins and Dylan Thomas. These poets represent in pure forms tendencies all of which are present in the Sonnets. There the singing line and the speaking voice, the sense and the sound of words, are always interacting. Performance requires gauging where the voice should be on a spectrum. And Yeats's 'music in the voice' need not mean a voice that is in conventional terms beautiful. The point can be enforced more obviously through sing-ing, where beauty of tone might appear more crucial. The great Greek-American soprano Maria Callas had a voice that was in many ways if not ugly then at least less than beautiful: it could be squally, thin, and harsh – 'failings' that, as signs of the presence of the fallibly human, were integral to its characteristic timbre and emotional immediacy. Beyond this, the voice's range of force and delicacy, and the singer's imaginative matching of sound quality to text, from fundamental tone to detailed inflection, were what made Callas's performances so expressive.

Analogies between poetry and music have a further implication for performance. It is a usual aspect of training in musical perform-ance that the player memorizes: as a result of constant practice, the music settles into the memory. Though you may continue to play from the score, memory helps the concentrated participation in performance that holds an audience's attention because the performer is wholly immersed in the music. Similarly, the effect of reading poems – whether for an actual listener or for the mind's ear – can be intensified by having a poem in the memory (while reading from the text) – so as to guide the (imagined) ear through the syntax, and to construct the poem's aural shapes in such a way as fully to inhabit its sequence of ideas and feelings. Gradual development of a poem in the memory is another aspect of living with it. It requires time and variety of circumstance, and a familiarity with the words themselves that is not primarily analytic. Wallace Stevens's fundamental desid-eratum – 'you must love the words . . . with all your capacity to love anything at all' – means not readily displacing the words with ideas about them. Memory has a role in this, as Ted Hughes implied in calling an anthology of favourite poems *By Heart*: memorizing – not by repeated pounding of isolated fragments, but by repeated engaged reading – is an aspect of learning to love.

How much the performance of poetry, and response to the per-formance of poetry, may engage the feelings by engaging the whole physical being is indicated by Plato's Homeric rhapsode, Ion.

> When I say something pitiable, my eyes brim with tears, and when I say something fearful or terrible, my hair stands straight on end from fear and my heart pounds. . . . I look down . . . from the stage and see [the spectators] weeping and gazing up at me fearfully, sharing the astonishment of what is being said.
>
> (Plato, *Ion*, §535c–e.)

From Ion's account of the physicality of emotion in performance Socrates extrapolates a set of relationships – poet-performer-audience – conceived in terms of quasi-physical connectedness, transmitting power as through rings connected to a lodestone. Ion and Socrates are discussing a particular and, in modern terms, an unusual kind of performance situation – the performance of epic to a large audience in a pre-literate society where poetry is conceived of predominantly in aural terms. Its nearest equivalent may be the Elizabethan popular theatre. The auditors of Donne's sermons who wept with the preacher indicate the readiness of Shakespeare's audience to participate responsively in performance. Shakespeare's Sonnets, of course, presuppose different performance expectations from his plays. If some of the 1609 publication were among the 'sugared sonnets among his private friends' reported by Francis Meres in 1598, evidently they were passed around for reading among a coterie. But any performance by an expressive speaker that is actually vocalized, public or private, actively engages the body: the lips, teeth, tongue, and throat are powerful vehicles of sensory awareness; the voice comes not just from the vocal chords and the resonators of the head, but from the lungs, the diaphragm muscles that support the breathing, and the whole network of muscles and tendons with which the diaphragm is connected. The performance of poetry in pre-literate societies is not unique in its physicality. Valéry's comments on reading poetry aloud were made in the context of performances of Racine in a style of French classical acting that survived well into the mid-twentieth century in which words were delivered with an intense physical relish of vocal tone, enjoyed in the mouth, even caressed. In a more muted manner the same fundamental style was used for reading lyric poetry. It is perfectly possible to find without extravagance an English equivalent of this – Wallace Stevens's 'loving the words . . . with all your capacity to love anything at all'. As a slow (very slow) reader of his own poetry Stevens positively exhibits it.

As part of a 'psychic physiology' about the 'systematic embodying of what is spiritual' Hegel comments on the physicality of voice and the individually expressive nature of vocal sound ('it is through the voice that a person makes known his inwardness, for he puts into it what he is') – though his interpretations of vocal tone are general and not sophisticated ('a pleasant voice indicates fineness of soul and a rough one crudity of feeling': Hegel, *Philosophy of Subjective Spirit*, trans. Petry, 2, 401). Proust comments similarly on the expressivity of voice, and, while he offers no specific interpretations, his sense of the potential range and subtlety of meanings is striking.

> Each [human voice] possesses more notes than the richest instrument of music. And the combinations in which it groups these notes are as inexhaustible as the richest variety of personalities. . . . The unique portrait of her individuality [each of the girls in an observed group] had been skilfully traced . . . as much by the inflections of her voice as by those of her face.

Proust's narrator generalizes from this observation of the particular group, presenting vocal tone as analogous to the evidence of character suggested by the face with a physicality that is erotic.

> Our intonation embodies our philosophy of life, what a person invariably says to himself about things. . . . Not only does a voice offer the same strange and sensuous surfaces as a face, it issues from that unknown, inaccessible region the mere thought of which sets the mind swimming with unattainable kisses.
>
> ('Place-Names: the Place', *Within a Budding Grove*, trans. Scott Moncrieff and Kilmartin, 969–70)

'Our intonation embodies our philosophy of life.' Intonation is the voice's equivalent of syntax in writing (Valéry [*Analects*]: 'syntax is a faculty of the soul') – the expressive shapes of how the individual uses language, governed in general terms by the language community as a whole, but capable of infinite minute variations that are individually expressive in proportion to the performative creativity of the speaker.

It is one thing to hear that the sounds of a voice imply meanings, another to give precise meanings to those sounds. Describing what one hears in a performing voice is highly problematic – what individual personality, what general cultural meanings, and why one responds to these as one does. The issues are more readily addressed with the singing than with the speaking voice. In the voice of Maria Callas one hears passion; in the voice of Kathleen Ferrier, purity; in the voice of Elizabeth Schwarzkopf, art – or the art that does not conceal art: calculation. Roland Barthes considered the meanings of voice with singers, and the meanings of sound in musical performance more generally. For him it is crucial to hear the presence of the body in the production of (vocal) tone – and, as with Ion, it is not only the body that performs: it is also the body that responds to performance.

> The 'grain' is the body in the voice as it sings . . . the limb as it performs. . . . I am determined to listen to my relation with the body of the man or woman singing or playing and that relation is erotic. . . . Leaving aside the voice, the 'grain' – or the lack of it – persists in instrumental music. . . . I shall not judge a performance according to the rules of interpretation . . . but according to the image of the body (the figure) given me. I can hear with certainty – the certainty of the body, of thrill – that the harpsichord playing of Wanda Landowska comes from her inner body and not from the petty digital scramble of so many harpsichordists. . . . As for piano music, I know at once which part of the body is playing – if it is the arm, too often, alas, muscled like a dancer's calves, the clutch of the finger-tips, . . . or if on the contrary it is the only erotic part of the pianist's body, the pad of the fingers whose 'grain' is so rarely heard.
>
> ('The Grain of the Voice')

This discussion of the performance of poetry set to music contrasts the 'grain' (presence of the body) in the voices of two singers, Charles Panzera and Dietrich Fischer-Dieskau. In Fischer-Dieskau Barthes heard breath and soul without body, fulfilment of the demands of an average culture, voice flattened into a paradoxically negative 'perfection' by the pressures of mass-market recording. In Panzera he heard the voluptuousness of vowels, the materiality of the body (tongue, glottis, teeth, mucous membranes, nose – not just the lungs) speaking in song its mother tongue, the language and its melody combined as a site of pleasure, the voice of a culture in which idiosyncrasy was not abolished by the demands of iterability. The particular judgements can be challenged. In relation to Fischer-Dieskau they seem to me foolish in the extreme, a mere preference for French over German. But the fundamental issues are: are some such general terms for understanding the meanings of vocal sound persuasive; do they suggest any comparable account of the speaking-performing voice?

When all that can be considered about the projection of form, meaning and feeling through the quasi-objective elements of sound-structure has been said, there is always in relation to the performance of poetry a judgement that can be rationalized only within limits. But accepting those limits, can one hear in the reading-performing voice – where the production of sound is not less, but less obviously of the whole body – similar individual or cultural meanings? And can one lead interpretative attention to the performing voice towards a heightened understanding of the poetry performed? Can what one aims for, and what one admires in the performance of poetry, both more deeply engage our understanding and be heard as an embodiment of meaning that conveys a poem in ways fully adequate to its range, depth and subtlety?

In seeking to understand the implications of vocal tone Barthes looked partly for cultural meanings. Like Hegel, and like Proust, he also looked for meanings more personal and individual. Most obviously one might hear in a speaking voice sex, class, and region. The interpretative power of voice is not dependent on any of these. Apart from what it registers culturally, a performing voice also suggests an implied personality ('implied': a performer may express passions entirely outside the range of the non-performing personality; how the performing voice relates to the non-performing self is not relevant). About this there will always be some element of mystery, but what the implied personality must finally convey is surely a human fullness able to engage completely with the subject matter of the poem in the forms in which the poem articulates it.

Consider two generally admired performers of Shakespeare whose voices seem to me to convey just such a human fullness, Richard Burton and Peggy Ashcroft.[2] Male/female; working-class/upper-middle class; regional accent (Welsh)/received pronunciation: they had nothing in common in terms of obvious vocal markers. They share technical competence in projecting every aspect of poetic form, an understanding of expressive conventions so practised as to have become intuitive. They are not, you feel, attending to anything technical. Their whole attention is on meaning and feeling. Burton was bi-lingual in English and Welsh: you hear that he was accustomed to a musical mode of speech. Ashcroft had difficulty with 'r': you hear a mild vocal impediment overcome. They are different in their degree of distance from the natural tones of colloquial speech. Burton, despite his bilingualism, and though his actual sounds are sometimes dialectal, is nearer in intonation to colloquial English. Ashcroft uses a less colloquially inflected, more singing tone, bringing out the structures of poetry to convey intensity of feeling in a more heightened way.

What more do we hear in the sound of Burton's voice? Beyond being a man's voice it is surely characteristically 'masculine' in force and emphasis – though it can be delicate as well as intense. It is a sensual voice, produced by the whole vocal mechanism – all the organs of the mouth and throat, but also, from deeper in the body (the pressure of the breath). His delivery is relatively naturalistic, often with colloquial intonation that brings out or follows syntactic rather than formal structures. His voice can participate without forcing in a wide range of feelings with variety of delivery, responding not only to heightened moments of drama (action, character) but also – and this produces the voice's most singing tones – to heightened formal and rhetorical structuration. It is the sound of a sensibility and intelligence able to engage completely with the subject matter of a given poem (poetic drama) in the forms in which the poetry articulates it.

What do we hear in the sound of Ashcroft's voice? For all her marking of form and rhetoric, essentially she finds the fundamental emotional tones for the given poetry's subjects without effects of art that are discontinuous with those of natural feeling. Her delivery is less naturalistic than Burton's, more obviously shaped by response to formal and rhetorical patterns. Characteristically she uses more extremes of vocal tone. She combines the speaking voice, with all its individual tones and the presence it registers of an engaged identity, with a voice transmuted towards song by responsiveness to the formal structures of art. In her individuality of inflection we hear rootedness in an idiosyncratic living being; in the singing line we hear art's transcendence of the purely personal. Even more than Burton, Ashcroft is a perfect exponent of Valéry's principles: a voice that, though it does not finally desert the expressivity of speech, is (as appropriate) on the verge of the complementary expressivity of song.

The performance of poetry, justifiably eager to escape the taint of recitation as an aspect of elocution, and properly keen to present itself democratically as potentially for everybody, tends to fight shy of speech-song. Of recorded readings of Shakespeare's Sonnets this inhibition can be heard at its strongest in the RSC/Penguin version, and in only slightly less extreme form with Richard Pascoe (Argo) and Alex Jennings (Naxos). The result is poetry read as though it were prose. Of course lineation is duly – even routinely – observed, but this does not make the prosaic poetic. It rather shows that a much more varied attention to structure is required for the voice to find the expressivity of poetic form. If there is music in these voices, I cannot hear it. As for Wordsworth's 'animated or impassioned recitation, adapted to the subject', the sound of visionary love or embittered betrayal is not here to be heard in tones I recognize. There may be some justification for prosaic delivery as a temporary stage, required to strip away actorly falsities or associations between poetry and

modes of reading aloud that are dead in ways socially specific (par-
sonical, mode of the lesson in church; pedagogical, mode of educational material). But fundamentally poetry-read-as-prose is disguised
Puritanism – a dislike of pleasure, colour, the exceptional. Boileau
reportedly remarked of Descartes that he had 'cut the throat of
poetry': by divorcing the mind from the body he cut off the intellect
from the emotions. The consequence was to make prose seem the
fully adequate discourse of the intelligence. Poetry presented as prose
is congruent with this: cut off from the bodily experience of emotion,
from song and from dance, the voice is deprived of the range of
colours that give so much of its expressivity.

Simon Callow (Hodder) is animated but actorly in projection;
syntax is usually well pointed by intonation, but the pace is wrong –
often simply too fast for the sense and movement of feeling to
register. Jack Edwards (Hyperion) too is instructive. Failing to find
intonations that point meaning, and giving attention to elocution in
such a way as to keep clear of natural feeling, these performances
should persuade anybody that there is no mystery to a sound start:
understand the meaning; convey it in tones natural to your own
mode of speech. This is the plain-fare method of David Tennant
(*From Shakespeare – with love*). It is much to be preferred, but better
than bad rather than positively good.

Where, then, can wisdom be found? Emotion experienced in and
through the performance of poetry, generated by the conjunction of
mental and physical concentration that reading aloud enforces, will
be audible in the voice. But there is no formula.

It all depends on . . . the natural *lingering* of the voice according to
the feeling – it is the hidden *emotional* pattern that makes poetry,
not the obvious form, . . . something as indefinite as expression in
the voice, carrying emotion. It doesn't depend on the ear, particularly, but on the sensitive soul. And the ear gets a habit, and
becomes master, when the ebbing and lifting emotion should be
master, and the ear the transmitter. . . . This is the constant war,

I reckon, between new expression and the habituated, mechanical transmitters and receivers of the human constitution.

(D. H. Lawrence, letter to Edward Marsh,
18 November 1913)

Well, the sensitive soul can only hear through the ear – but one sees Lawrence's point: ear-minded criteria will be ready-made; they are not what the soul listens for. It scarcely matters that Lawrence is thinking about 'new expression' historically: old forms should always be heard as they were when new. Can there be an emotional pattern not involved with a poem's form? Here too Lawrence is surely right: patterns the fully engaged emotional intelligence can hear may not be entirely those the mind has been taught to see. Reading poetry aloud has to be minutely responsive in the moment – the voice used 'according to the feeling', sounding the whole being, the poem engaging all the capacities of intellect and feeling through the voice. When there is some compromise of what is genuinely alive in the moment by what can be recognized as an effect of contrivance or routine, attention slackens and the poem goes dead.

Performing returns a poem from the fixity of print to the fluidity of the particular occasion of its saying. In never taking the same form twice, the spoken word (like the hand-written word) is a human product congruent, as the endlessly reproducible printed text is not, with actual experiences of reading: it is always different. On this analogy recorded readings are like good reproductions of handwriting – lithographs, with the indentations characteristic of script; not photographs, with the smooth surface characteristic of mechanical reproduction. Though a recording will not vary with the occasion of its reproduction, what it preserves is potentially a real trace of full human presence.

Probably no reading of the Sonnets could entirely satisfy Lawrence's demanding criteria, but among recorded readings Gielgud (Harper-Collins) at least dares to sing. This is so radical a contradiction of contemporary norms as to be valuable in itself; and though Gielgud does not quite have Peggy Ashcroft's way of combining a singing intonation that gives aural shape to form with a colloquial intonation that points meaning, he has a lilt all his own, and conveys the singing line that is the root of this poetry. You hear both the experience of acting Romeo and Othello, and a natural affinity for the subject of the WH poems. (The period of the recording [1962] coincided with Gielgud's first meetings with Martin Hensler, thirty years his junior and thereafter his lifelong companion.)

Some of the most satisfying readings are those that – like Judi Dench on Derek Jarman's soundtrack – take the poems slowly, allowing Lawrence's 'natural lingering of the voice according to the feeling'. The actors in Kevin Billington's television films (Courthouse/Goldcrest) each deliver their sonnet twice, with the two readings separated by commentary by one of a varied group of writers and intellectuals. The two readings are in different (Elizabethan/Jacobean) costumes and settings – so the second is not simply a re-showing but is actually a new performance, sometimes significantly varied from the first. The tele-visual medium means that the performers' eyes, face and body, as well as voice, are all engaged in expression. This has the simple effect of slowing delivery, but also (perhaps because the whole body is engaged) prompting a more varied use of voice; and because the poems are spoken from memory, characteristically the performances give a sense of the poem being integrated with the performers' whole vocal mechanism and thoroughly interiorized.

The best of the audio anthologies, *When Love Speaks* (EMI), is performed by generations of RADA graduates from the 1920s to the 1990s, so gives a finely various picture of Shakespeare performance styles in British theatre through the twentieth century. Its successes are illustrative: meaning, form, tone are key. Alan Bates ('Tired with all these', 66) is a demonstration. He finds the right fundamental tone ('tired with' taken to mean 'sturdily resentful at the wrong, injustice, sin of . . . '), with expressive variations (gruff contempt for the authority of censors; sarcasm for doctor-like folly), and variations of pace to bring out form and to bring out sense (different kinds of wrong grouped; breaks before the sestet and before the turn in thought of the final line). John Hurt ('Those lips that love's own hand did make', 145) shows how to shape the play of syntax against form (across quatrains and line endings) to build the extended sentence that culminates in release from pain, 'not you' ('I hate . . . not you'). Edward Fox's fruitily-voiced 'Be wise as thou art cruel' (140) is nicely juxtaposed with the ultra-modern plainness of Zoe Waites, who points sense expressively by intonation and pace in a sonnet of complex antitheses ('Since I left you': 113). Richard Johnson wryly accepting love's deceits in 'When my love swears' (138) shows how a play of tones more usual on stage may suit a sonnet – rightly, since the poems are in several senses 'dramatic': they involve conflict of characters, internal conflicts in the speaker, implied narrative 'off stage', and intimate immediacy ('now, / Now') as of an action evolving in the present.

The successes are complemented by illustrative error: chopping up the syntax so as to produce the mode of Peter Quince ('all for your delight we are not here'); failure to convey sense (phrasing antitheses as parallels: Marianne Jean-Baptiste, 15.7); failure to understand syntax ('she' as subject, not object: Alan Rickman, 130.14); failure to hear rhythm (subtracting syllables – humorously notable when 'stretchèd metre' is contracted to 'stretch'd': Richard Attenborough, 17.12) – though with failure to hear rhythm there is nothing so bizarre as Al Pacino (Airplay Audio), reading 'possessèd' for 'possessed' (29.6) when the word rhymes with 'least'. For the quintessence of Hamlet's 'too tame', a grand defiance of time (19, David Harewood) is read in the same fundamental (prosaic) tones as a melancholy recognition of transience as all-powerful (12, Martin Jarvis).

For performance of the singing line it is instructive to compare Juliet Stevenson and Anton Lesser (*From Shakespeare – with love*). Stevenson reads with myriad minute inflections, not expressive in detail, but with the tone constantly various, mobile and fluctuating.

This is the Lotte Lehmann style in song: the sound of flexible entire engagement, art so thoroughly digested as to appear almost artless. Lesser (reading Sonnet 65) colours more precisely: 'batt'ring days . . . time decays' (super-emphatic plosives); 'Where [pause], alack'; 'O none [double pause], unless this [higher pitch, for wonder] miracle have might'. This is the Elizabeth Schwarzkopf style: its virtues do not include the impression of natural feeling. In song, where the voice is fully a musical instrument, a great deal of inflexion and colour can be, and so can sound, spontaneous. It is the equivalent of the string-player colouring the musical line with more or less vibrato, more or less pressure of the bow, techniques that become intuitive and so can be exercised by the ear in relation to the feelings in the moment. But in poetry, when the voice is, though not simply speaking, not singing either – the natural speaking voice raised towards the level of singing; speech on the verge of song – then too much colour can upset that delicate balance. For me, Lesser is too much: it is the sound of artifice, not of art; what T. S. Eliot means by not trusting the words. Attention is deflected from the poem to the performer.

Let no moralist or utilitarian persuade that poetry must have a purpose beyond pleasure. Pleasure is its own purpose. But if there are purposes to reading poetry beyond pleasure one is surely to find out who you might become, to inhabit imaginatively verbal structures through which you can think and feel in ways other than those dictated by the accidents of time, place, and circumstance. Finding one's own reading voice is potentially a major route to this. Individual vocalization that is fully responsive to the whole being of the reader and to the full meanings of the poem is a critical activity of the first order. Yeats and Stevens give the alpha and omega: a fundamental tone appropriate to the subject; the shapes of syntax and the shapes of form; pleasure in the language. Understanding in what the expressive sounds of verse consist; finding the music that can convey those sounds in the natural capabilities of your voice; loving with all your capacity the words, the images, the rhythms, the ideas.

Text Notes

1. Eliot's idea of the 'auditory imagination' is endorsed and explored by Seamus Heaney in *Englands of the Mind*, *Finders Keepers: Selected Prose, 1971–2001*, London: Faber, 2002.
2. Burton's Shakespeare reading is best sampled in performances of *The Rape of Lucrece* and the title role in *Coriolanus* (both directed by Howard Sackler, Caedmon). Ashcroft's Shakespeare recordings include performances of Lucrece in *The Rape of Lucrece* and Beatrice in *Much Ado about Nothing* (both directed by George Rylands, Argo), Queen Margaret in *Richard III* and Paulina in *The Winter's Tale* (both directed by Howard Sackler, Caedmon). She recorded four of the Sonnets for a general anthology of poetry (Caedmon, 1956).

Coda

Dwelling in the feelings: emotions fundamental to the poems experienced imaginatively through a variety of forms of embodiment. Dwelling in the words: precise articulations of the poems as these are given aural form by the living voice. These are opposite approaches to the same end – greater emotional engagement with the poetry. Their value is not dependent on the poetry's subject or its forms.

But when the subject is love that cannot be directly expressed, or can be expressed only within limits, it may also be that creation is a way of making love, and performance may have a special relation to Eros displaced. In all the work discussed here as analogous to Shakespeare's Sonnets there is an element of erotic displacement. Alcibiades testifies to Socrates's chastity: he also identifies as crucial to Socrates's dialogues with young men the concealed stimulus of deflected desire. Desire deflected in Michelangelo's poetry and drawing is an overt subject. But here too it also has a covert presence. Michelangelo's plea (on a drawing from the 1520s) that he not be asked to draw 'perchè e' non c'è el Perino' (because [Gherardo] Perini is not present) indicates the importance for Michelangelo of the creative stimulus provided by male beauty ('perchè . . . Perino': Luitpold Dussler, *Die Zeichnungen des Michelangelo: Kritischer Katalog*, Berlin, 1959, D439). Engaging Tommaso dei Cavalieri in the creation of a drawing with an erotic subtext by requesting guidance about its composition (*Phaëton*: Buck, §4) has a congruent implication. Like Mann's Socrates, Michelangelo is here surely a 'sly wooer'. For the teacher taught by his pupil, drawing contrives covert erotic reciprocation. Whether by constructing sexual meanings or submitting to

their negation hardly matters: for the expression of love self-abnegation will do quite as well as self-assertion. For Aschenbach similarly,
to write is to make love. Since 'Eros dwells in language', prose fully
adequate to Mann's originary hymnic impulse can be the Zeus-eagle
to Tadzio's Ganymede. It is not (or not only) a matter of content: it
is texture and rhythm that give voice to the experience of engaged
desire. (At particularly intense moments Mann's prose assumes the
pulse of the Homeric hexameter – an effect the reader can experience
without any knowledge of classical poetry, though obviously it is
more likely to be felt through actual voicing, or at least by imagining
the words spoken.) And who is more the covert wooer than Britten? –
finding Eros in the musical equivalent of the presence of Gherardo
and co-creation with Tommaso, by writing operatic roles for boys he
loved (for David Hemmings, Miles in *The Turn of the Screw*), even
when they had no training as singers (for David Spenser, Harry in
Albert Herring). *The Angelic Conversation* may seem an exception
here, which in part it is: matching straightforwardly homoerotic
images of longing and fulfilment with aural realizations of the
Sonnets that smooth out their complexities of tone, its meanings
(however obscure) are apparently on the surface. The film's narrative
and tonal simplifications are indices of how, with many of the poems,
an ambivalent language of love, friendship, passion and sexuality can
be read as covert encodings that the film's overt agenda ignores. But
even here Eros is in the medium: Jarman began simply by miscellane-
ous filming of two young men he found attractive. In the film as
completed, the camera's gaze, as it dwells on the faces and bodies of
Phillip and Paul, imitates the yearning eye of desire.

It is tempting to think that there may be some congruence between
these acts of creation that are covert acts of love and the reading and
performance of at least the more intimate of the Sonnets, that the
performance of this poetry may be a new release of the suppressed.
The voice fully responsive to the experience of the poem in the
moment of reading (vide Lawrence: 'in the voice . . . the ebbing and
lifting emotion'): this may well realise aurally and release for the

reader and the listener emotions that are barely recognized, or are recognized only in and through performance. Like Stevens' 'nobility' ('intelligence, desire for life'), there is often more to be heard in the overtones of poetry than can be brought confidently into consciousness. The grand melancholy of many of the WH Sonnets may well seem to those with ears to hear what Mann heard in the poetry of Michelangelo: the music of suppressed desire. Then there are qualities in the half-covert gift of love through creation that have affinities with all reading and performance – with the reader's ideal engagement with the poem (manner of Wallace Stevens: 'love with all your capacity to love'); with a criticism that approaches depths through surfaces (manner of Susan Sontag: 'in place of a hermeneutics an erotics'); with the performer's engagement of the mind-body feeling-intelligence through the voice (manner of Valéry: 'the tenderness, the violence'); and with the listener's sense of the meanings of vocal tone drawn from the whole body (manner of Barthes: 'the relation [with the performer] is erotic'). Eros may be present in the voice in the manner of Burton – more colloquial, more individual, half-revealed. It may be present in the manner of Ashcroft – more incantatory, more impersonal, half-concealed. How this works, if it works at all, will depend on the reader's imaginative affinity with the subject and ability to discover and convey through the vocal personality a sensibility and intelligence engaged with the subject in the forms in which the poem articulates it. Queer poetry is not only for queer readers. Far from it. The feelings that can be discovered through the voice working experimentally with a poem are not simply those the reader brings. Voicing a poem will often be an encounter with what was previously beyond the self – one way or another, a result of dwelling in the feelings and dwelling in the words.

Sources and References

Prologue

Friedrich Nietzsche, *Twilight of the Idols*, in *Twilight of the Idols and The Anti-Christ*, trans. R. J. Hollingdale, Harmondsworth: Penguin, 1968. Friedrich Schlegel, *Kritische Fragmente*, *Kritische Schrifte*, ed. Wolfdietrich Rasch, München: Hanser, 1956. Yeats, 'Samhain: 1902', *Explorations*, London: Macmillan, 1962. Eliot's letter to Stephen Spender, from Spender, '*Remembering Eliot*', Allen Tate (ed.), *T. S. Eliot: the Man and his Work*, London: Chatto, 1967. Susan Sontag, *Against Interpretation: and Other Essays*, New York: Farrar, 1966.

Dwelling in the Feelings

The Sonnets are quoted from the edition of Katherine Duncan-Jones, Arden 3, London: Thomson Learning, 1997. I have also particularly consulted the editions of W. G. Ingram and Theodore Redpath (London: Hodder, 1964), John Kerrigan (Harmondsworth: Penguin, 1986), and Colin Burrow (Oxford: Oxford University Press, 2002).

Introduction

Nietzsche, *Daybreak: Thoughts on the Prejudices of Morality*, trans. R. J. Hollingdale, Cambridge: Cambridge University Press, 1982.

Plato

Plato, *Symposium*, translated with an introduction and notes by Robin Waterfield, Oxford: Oxford University Press, 1994. Plato, *Phaedrus*, translated with an introduction and notes by Robin Waterfield, Oxford:

Oxford University Press, 2002. The standard account of the context is K. J. Dover, *Greek Homosexuality*, Cambridge, MA: Harvard, 1978; new edition, 1989. Notable modern discussions include: Martha Nussbaum, *The Fragility of Goodness: Luck and Ethics in Greek Tragedy and Philosophy*, Cambridge: Cambridge University Press, 1986, revised edition 2001 (chapters 6 and 7); A. W. Price, *Love and Friendship in Plato and Aristotle*, Oxford: Oxford University Press, 1989 (chapters 2 and 3); Michel Foucault, *The Use of Pleasure* (The History of Sexuality, vol. 2, 1984), trans. Robert Hurley, Harmondsworth: Penguin, 1987 (parts 4 and 5).

Michelangelo

Editions of the Italian texts of Michelangelo's Rime with translations include those of James M. Saslow, *The Poetry of Michelangelo: An Annotated Translation*, New Haven: Yale University Press, 1991; and Christopher Ryan, *Michelangelo: The Poems*, London: Dent, 1996. I quote from Ryan's texts and translations. Michelangelo's letters are quoted from *The Letters of Michelangelo*, trans. E. H. Ramsden, 2 volumes, Stanford, CA: Stanford University Press, 1963. Vasari's life of Michelangelo is quoted from *The Life of Michelangelo Buonarroti*, trans. George Bull, London: Folio Society, 1971. For paintings and drawings see Frank Zöllner et al., *Michelangelo, 1475–1564: Complete Works*, Köln: Taschen, 2007; and *Michelangelo's Dream*, ed. Stephanie Buck, London: Courtauld Gallery, 2010 (a catalogue accompanying an exhibition of the Cavalieri presentation drawings). On the date of birth of Tommaso dei Cavalieri (arguing that Tommaso was born in 1519 or 1520) see G. Panofsky-Soergel, 'Postscriptum to Tommaso Cavalieri', *Scritti di storia dell'arte in onore di Roberto Salvini*, ed. C. de Benedictis, Firenze: Sansoni, 1984, 399–405. Michael Rocke, *Forbidden Friendships: Homosexuality and Male Culture in Renaissance Florence* (Oxford: Oxford University Press, 1996) gives an account of aspects of the context in which Michelangelo grew up.

Mann

Quotations from the novella are from *Der Tod in Venedig*, ed. T. J. Reed, Oxford: Clarendon, 1971, and *'Death in Venice' and Other Stories*, trans.

David Luke, New York: Bantam, 1988, 2008 (to which page references are given in the text). Quotations from Mann's diaries and letters are from *Thomas Mann Diaries: 1918–39*, selected Hermann Kesten, trans. Richard and Clara Winston, London: Robin Clark, 1984, and *The Letters of Thomas Mann*, selected and translated by Richard and Clara Winston, Harmondsworth: Penguin, 1975. Translations have been checked where possible (not everything has been published) against the German editions of the *Tagebücher, 1918–43*, ed. Peter de Mendelssohn (5 vols, Frankfurt: Fisher, 1977–82), *1944–50*, ed. Inge Jens (2 vols, Frankfurt: Fischer, 1986, 1989) and the *Briefe*, ed. Erika Mann, 3 vols, Frankfurt: Fischer, 1961–65. Translations from letters or diaries not in these volumes are from Hermann Kurzke, *Thomas Mann: Life as a Work of Art*, trans. Leslie Willson, London: Allen Lane, 2002. Other quotations are from Mann's *Essays of Three Decades*, trans. H. T. Lowe-Porter, London: Secker, 1959 ('Kleist's *Amphitryon*' and *'Platen'*) and Mann's *Gesammelte Werke*, Frankfurt: Fischer, 12 vols, 1960 ('Die Erotik Michelangelo's', vol. 9, 783–93).

Britten

Death in Venice, libretto by Myfanwy Piper, vocal score, London: Faber, 1973; orchestral score, London: Faber, 1979. David Herbert (ed.), *The Operas of Benjamin Britten*, London: Hamish Hamilton, 1979 (complete librettos, designs for first productions, essays by some of Britten's principal collaborators). Donald Mitchell, *Death in Venice*, Cambridge Opera Handbooks, Cambridge: Cambridge University Press, 1987. John Bridcut, *Britten's Children*, London: Faber, 2006. Performances. Audio: conducted by Stuart Bedford, supervised by Britten, with Peter Pears as Aschenbach (1974). Film dir. Tony Palmer, set on location in Venice, conducted by Stuart Bedford, with John Shirley-Quirk as the Traveller et al., James Bowman as Apollo (both from the original cast), and Robert Gard as Aschenbach (1981).

Jarman

Derek Jarman, *The Angelic Conversation*, 1985, BFIVD724. 'On *Imaging October*, Dr. Dee and Other Matters: An Interview with Derek Jarman',

Simon Field and Michael O'Pray, *Afterimage* (London), 12 (autumn 1985), 40–58. Derek Jarman, *Kicking the Pricks* (Diary, volume 4), Woodstock, NY: Overlook Press, 1987. Chris Lippard (ed.), *By Angels Driven: the Films of Derek Jarman*, Trowbridge: Flicks, 1995. Tony Peake, *Derek Jarman*, London: Abacus, 2001. William Pencak, *The Films of Derek Jarman*, Jefferson, NC: McFarland, 2002. Steve Dillon, *Derek Jarman and Lyric Film: the Mirror and the Sea*, Austin: University of Texas Press, 2004. Rowland Wymer, *Derek Jarman*, British Film Makers, Manchester: Manchester University Press, 2005.

Dwelling in the Words

W. H. Auden, *The Dyer's Hand*, London: Faber, 1963. *The English Auden: Poems, Essays and Dramatic Writings, 1927–1939*, ed. Edward Mendelson, London: Faber, 1977. Roland Barthes, *Image – Music – Text*, essays selected and translated by Stephen Heath, London: Fontana, 1977. Basil Bunting, *Descant on Rawthey's Madrigal: Conversations with Basil Bunting*, ed. Jonathan Williams, Lexington, KY: Gnomon, 1968. *Collected Letters of Samuel Taylor Coleridge*, ed. Earl Leslie Griggs, 6 vols, Oxford: Clarendon, 1956–71. T. S. Eliot, *The Use of Poetry and the Use of Criticism*, London: Faber, 1933. T. S. Eliot, *On Poetry and Poets*, London: Faber, 1957. 'T. S. Eliot Answers Questions', Ranjee Shahani, *John O'London's Weekly*, LVIII.1369 (19 August 1949), 497–98. G. W. F. Hegel, *Philosophy of Subjective Spirit*, ed. and trans. M. J. Petry, 3 vols, Dortrecht: Riebel, 1978. *The Letters of Gerard Manly Hopkins to Robert Bridges*, ed. Claude Colleer Abbott, London: Oxford, 1935. Ted Hughes, *By Heart*, London: Faber, 1999. Plato, *Ion, Hippias Minor, Laches, Protagoras*, trans. R. E. Allen, New Haven: Yale, 1996. *The Literary Essays of Ezra Pound*, ed. T. S. Eliot, London: Faber, 1954. Marcel Proust, *Within a Budding Grove*, in *Remembrance of Things Past*, trans. C. K. Scott Moncrieff and Terence Kilmartin, 3 vols, Harmondsworth: Penguin, 1983 (vol. 2). Jonathan Rée, *I See a Voice*, London: HarperCollins, 1999. Wallace Stevens, 'The Noble Rider and the Sounds of Words', *The Necessary Angel: Essays on Reality and the Imagination*, New York: Random House, 1951; *Opus Posthumous*, ed. Samuel French Morse, New York: Knopf, 1957. Paul Valéry, *Collected Works*, ed. Jackson Matthews. 15 vols, London: Routledge,

1957–75; (vol. 7), *On the Art of Poetry*, trans. Denise Folliot, intro. T. S. Eliot. W. J. B. Owen and Jane Smyser (eds.), *The Prose Works of William Wordsworth*, 3 vols, Oxford: Clarendon, 1974. W. B. Yeats, 'Samhain: 1906. Literature and the Living Voice', *Explorations*, London: Macmillan, 1962.

Recorded Readings

The Marlowe Society of Cambridge, dir. George Rylands, Argo/British Council (ten anonymous readers, including Rylands, 1958). John Gielgud, HarperCollins (originally Caedmon, 1963 [about 120 sonnets]). Richard Pascoe, Argo (originally London Records, 1984). A (largely) RSC group, – Peter Egan, Peter Orr, Bob Peck, and Michael Williams, Penguin Audiobooks (1995). Jack Edwards, Helios/Hyperion (1988–91). Simon Callow, Hodder Headline (1995). Alex Jennings, Naxos (1997). Helen Vendler, published with her book on the Sonnets (Yale, UP, 1999). A group, including Claire Bloom, Patrick Stewart, and Al Pacino, Airplay Audio (1999). *When Love Speaks*, readings of about 50 sonnets by several generations of RADA graduates, EMI/RADA (2002). *From Shakespeare – with love,* readings of about half of the Sonnets by various actors, including David Tenant, Juliet Stevenson, and Anton Lesser, Naxos (2009).

Readings and critical presentations (Courthouse Films, UK; Goldcrest Films, US), 1983–84; directed by Kevin Billington, readings by Claire Bloom, Roger Rees, Jane Lapotaire, Ben Kingsley, and other actors; commentary by Stephen Spender, Gore Vidal, Leslie Fiedler, Arnold Wesker, and other writers. US DVD, ISBN 978–1-4213–6346–2. (13 Sonnets)

Index

Only the more extended discussions of particular Sonnets are referenced.